LIFE,
and THAT'S Okay

By: Angela D. Borkowski

Second Edition 2020

Copyright © 2019 by Angela D Borkowski

All rights reserved
Including the right of reproduction
In whole or in part in any form

Contents

Introduction	4
It Starts with You!	8
Having a Bad Day—Do You Have to, Though?	12
Do You Judge?	20
Judgment Day	31
Why Do We Do What We Do?	38
Why Is the Past Hard to Let Go?	44
Finding Out	48
Dating	62
Jealousy	74
Marriage	79
Money	92
Parenting	100
Being a Good Role Model	108
Thinking the Grass Is Greener Over There	117
Are You The Receiver Or The Caller?	127
Menopause	134
We Are Daily Growing	139

This book is for all maturing ages. It's never too young to learn about Life, and THAT'S Okay. I have been emotionally hurt too many times in my life, or I've seen people struggling through life being hurt, and the reason we all hurt so badly is because we are still growing and don't understand life. It's part of growing.

I'll be honest—I've never been a big reader of books, but my paternal grandmother read and read and read. She would send me newspaper articles and books with important words circled or highlighted. I always wanted to learn to read and be excited about reading as much as she was. I knew knowledge was in these books. I was always so excited, looking at them with butterflies in my stomach at the thought what they may hold inside. But I'd open them and often lose interest. It wasn't because they were boring—it was because I struggled to read. When I had kids of my own, I realized they were having the same struggle. One day, we went with my husband on a business trip out of state. I was watching TV, and this documentary came on about dyslexia. My mouth dropped. I thought, "That was me in school. That is me now. That's my kids." After having the kids tested, we found out the older two had dyslexia, which they inherited from me, which I then learned I'd gotten from my dad. The wonder of a dyslexic brain is so amazing, and I wouldn't want to have gone through life without this gift. Having dyslexia isn't just about reading. The brain of a person with dyslexia is a gift on many aspects. We can alter and create perceptions, we're more curious about things, we think mostly with pictures in our head instead of words, we're highly aware of our environment, we have a vivid imagination, and can experience thought as reality. However, it would have been nice to know I had dyslexia when I was a child to help explain why school was hard and why reading was such a struggle. After learning I had dyslexia and learning about everything dyslexia is, I really grew over the last several years. I no longer felt stupid. There finally was an answer to why I struggled academically learning out of a school book. It explained why I was able to retain information when things were taught hands on to me. Just the knowledge of knowing why reading was so hard for me made me want to learn more, because I wasn't stupid or couldn't, I just have a special gift that I had to learn to work with. I learned to love reading and stay focused when doing so. It also helped when my youngest child was born, who I believe does not have dyslexia. He wanted me to read to him at night when he was a baby and into his third year, when sadly he just didn't want me to sit by his bed and read to him anymore. When I would read to him he didn't want baby stories, he wanted chapter books, and he'd lie in his bed with a look of wonder and delight on his face as I would end up reading about 30–50 pages to him each night before he fell asleep. I got to read all those childhood classics I'd always wanted to read because of my son, and it was amazing.

What was the point of me telling you all that? Well, I know I'm not the only one out there who struggles with reading. And guess what? THAT'S OKAY. The way to get better is just to keep doing it. Maybe you can only handle reading for five or ten minutes here or there. That's way better then not picking up a book at all. Your brain is constantly learning and wanting to learn.

This book is about learning life and learning that it's Okay. So pick up this book and read it for a short time, or be like my mother, who would sit down for hours and read for as long as time allowed. Get out your pencil or highlighters and feel free to comment on or highlight important lines that mean something to you or make you think of someone with whom you may want to share this book, just like my grandmother would have.

It Starts with You!

Have you ever realized that you alone could affect thousands, even millions of people? When my husband and I were newly dating and first married, he told me that when he and I had a bad day, it affected him emotionally, which in turn, would change how he was going to handle things at work. But if we had an amazing day and he went to work on a high from love, then people at work were probably going to be able to get away with a little more silliness.

My husband affects how I feel all the time. If he's happy and in a good mood, so am I. If he's sulky, it puts me in a sour mood too. Sadly, it's my kids who normally see that side of me because I become short-tempered with them.

Let's go back to my husband's work. This isn't a true story but rather an example of how we affect each other. Imagine he and I just spent an amazing date together, and he went into work at a retail store, and a lot of the employees were acting silly and not 100% following the rules. They threw a ball in the store, and he casually caught it and threw it back, and he nicely corrected them, saying, "Looks like fun. Now let's get back to unloading and stocking the shelves, and then we can play ball on your break." Then because Joe Smith got to laugh and be silly at work, he went home in a good mood and told his wife, "I know you have been working so hard here. You should go out with your friends," and he stayed home and watched the kids. Mrs. Smith went out with her girlfriends, and she was just glowing to them about how sweet her husband was to give her a break from the kids and housework. She encouraged one of her friends to realize how lucky she was that her own husband had suggested her to go out, so that friend went home to give her husband a great big hug and a kiss, and they spent alone time together. The next morning, the friend's husband woke up and headed to work in a really good mood, thinking about the night before with his wife . . . and so on.

Now imagine my husband and I got into an argument right before he went to work. Even worse, we didn't get to finish it before he left. He went to work on edge, frustrated about the lingering fight, and Joe Smith was throwing a ball in the store on company time. Instead of being nice about it, my husband called Joe back to his office and wrote him up. Joe had evil thoughts about my husband and left the office complaining to his coworkers, who talked to other coworkers, and of course the story changed a few times, and my husband became the villain. Joe went home to his wife and kids, and she was happily waiting to surprise him with his favorite dinner. But he was moody and stomped around the house. He told his wife he wasn't hungry. "Daddy, Daddy," the kids screamed as they jumped on him, and he said, "Kids just leave me alone. Daddy had a bad day at work." So the kids were sad and begged for more attention, which lead to Joe screaming at them to knock it off and go to bed early. Mrs. Smith got depressed because she worked hard to make her husband his favorite meal, and he came home and was short with her and refused to eat. He lay on the couch watching TV, playing on his phone, and ignoring his family. There're many other Joe Smiths out there, so imagine 30 of them had the same experience and then gave the same to their families of four . . . and so on.

Do you see how everyone can affect everyone else and how it increases exponentially? So the next time you're having a bad day, stop and try to refocus yourself, or at least don't lash out at others.

Remember, we all have bad days. Instead of letting that negative energy in, try to let it go so it can't bring you down. It is hard when you spend time with someone who's irritable and can't get away from it, such as a husband or wife coming home from work in a bad mood.

The opposite spouse should be the other's rock, listen, and hopefully get that person out of his or her funk.

∞ ∞ ∞

Having a Bad Day— Do You Have to, Though?

I went to the Department of Motor Vehicles (DMV) office one day. I'd bought a shark car. Yes, you read that right—a car designed to look like a shark. My husband had jokingly said, "You wanted the car, you can register the car," but seriously, he wasn't going to spend all day registering the car that I wanted. I headed to the DMV office at 10:30 a.m. and left at 2 p.m. Yes, three and a half hours later, I walked out. Most people would have been anxious, frustrated, or mad. Well, I struck up a conversation with an older lady who was probably in her 70s or 80s. She was number 74 and I was number 75, and they were on number 27. She was frustrated that she'd forgotten to register her car to get the sticker in the mail. I, of course, started to joke about the movie, Zootopia, that has the sloths for the DMV people. We spoke of our husbands—how hers was probably glad she was out of the house for a bit because he got to watch his old Western movies that she doesn't care for. I told her, "I bet you'd rather be watching an old Western movie than sitting here waiting." She chuckled. We watched and talked about the poor little toddlers who also had to endure the wait, including the one who wanted tater tots and the one strapped to a dinosaur leash screaming because he wanted out of that place. Then the leashed toddler found a girl his age and started to flirt with her, and she loved it, but then she decided to run free because she wasn't on a leash, and she taunted him by running, laughing, and sticking her tongue out at him. The older lady and I just laughed. She and I both understood these poor kids were trapped here waiting like us with their family. It wasn't their choice to be stuck in a room full of people doing nothing but waiting. The guy to my right was grumpy. He just huffed a grumpy bear huff because the kids were being loud. We were all kids once, and not one of us was good all the time. Sometimes, parents don't have a choice not to bring their kids. I took my middle son once to the DMV office when he was a toddler. Needless to say, that's why my husband did most of the other DMV trips by himself.

    This lady and I continued to talk, laugh, and smile. The DMV ladies kept looking over at us as the hours passed, and some left for lunch for an hour and came back, and there we still sat. As this lady and I continued to talk, we laughed more and more. One lady who'd sat to my right after the grumpy old man had left didn't seem to be having as much fun as us, so she got up and sat in some quiet seats staring at nothing. But others who had been sitting there for a long time—some longer than us—actually got out of their seats and came to join the older lady and me because we were having a ball, killing time, talking, and laughing. The next thing you knew, everyone in our whole section of seats was acting as if they were at a ball game. Each time a person's number was called, we cheered. When they called a number but the person had already left, we cheered even more. Number 47 got called, which belonged to a lady who was going on a cruise that night. She walked up to the lady at the desk and pointed over to us, and we heard her say in a joking manner, "Those people over there are unhappy with how long they have to wait and are saying bad things about you. I, however, think you are doing an amazing job." While she was up there, she kept turning around and looking at us still having fun. The older lady yelled at her, "Why do you keep looking at us?" Number 47 replied, "Because I feel those dagger eyes in my back." I chimed in, "Well, if you didn't throw us under the bus with the DMV lady, we wouldn't be giving you dagger eyes." It was a fun three-and-a-half hours. When it was my turn, the crowd was cheering, and I danced my way up with raise-the-roof hands in the air. The DMV lady was the sweetest girl, and she was really happy because we'd helped create a stress-free environment. She was even more excited when she found out she was getting me a new title for a shark car.

Life is all about how we look at things. How we respond to things. How we want to feel. I could have sat there for three-and-a-half hours on my cell phone, frustrated with the fact that I was just waiting. I could have gotten mad at how slow the DMV girls were. But the reality is that they were doing their jobs. Yes, I wish there had been a faster solution, but life isn't always supposed to be fast. We have just been so spoiled over the years with the fast pace of life and technology that we expect that when we want something, we should get it now! Sometimes, in life, you need to slow down, put down your cell phone, and look at your surroundings. Say hello to a stranger sitting next to you and get to know a different lifestyle. It was amazing to learn that when this elderly lady first got her driver's license, she wasn't even there. Her husband signed the paper for her when he was getting his. The funny part was that he had forgotten her birthday and put down the wrong date. She said, "I figured that means he needs to buy me gifts twice a year for my birthday." It wasn't a big thing in the '50s or '60s when she got her license.

When my dad was alive, he didn't have computers or smartphones to surf the web. But he knew everyone who lived in all the houses we used to drive by, and he knew almost their entire life stories. He would stop and introduce himself to people and strike up conversations and listen to what they had to say and learn so many things from them. That's what we need to do. Instead of having a bad day, turn it around, open your eyes, and look around you. Try making a new friend, even if it's only a five-minute friend. The human body is designed to communicate face-to-face with someone, not just through a cell phone. Getting 200 likes on a photo isn't the same feeling as talking and laughing with another human in person.

The next time you are stuck somewhere waiting, look up from your phone and say, "Hello" to the person near you. Sometimes, you may need to nudge that person with a little more than a hello, but try it. It will lift up your spirits and probably those of the people around you even more. People want to be happy, and they will be drawn toward the happiness of others.

Maybe you were working today and a customer started yelling at you. Maybe that person had the right to yell because something went totally wrong. But many times, people yell at people because they are in a bad mood and think this will make them feel better. This is normally not the case, though. Yelling at someone just puts someone else in a bad mood or hurts someone. I was in customer service for several years, and I had my share of people yelling at me. Sometimes, people in life will still walk away mad just because they didn't know how to switch into a good mood. But most of the time when people who would yell at me, I'd just listen and hear why they were actually upset. It was usually something so minor, but they had worked themselves up for no reason. I would continue to smile and help resolve the issue, and they would walk away smiling, sometimes even apologizing for getting so upset. We all get mad from time to time, which normally leads to a bad day.

What most people need to learn is:
A: Not let others get to us;
B: Listen to the real reason people are upset; and
C: Help those people the best we can.

Often, people in a bad mood probably aren't even mad at you or for the things they are yelling at you about. A lot of things may have built up, and they just needed to finally explode, and you just happened to be the one they exploded on. Remember, if you did nothing wrong, or you made a minor mistake you can fix, don't take it personally and make it your bad day too. Try to understand when these people are exploding on you to just smile and help fix their bad days.

Maybe you and a loved one are fighting. I have learned over the years to just stop talking before I say something I really don't mean and breathe. The other day, I was doing some research and came across a new technique that really made sense in every step. Richard Williams had posted a YouTube video. You may know him better by his stage name Prince Ea. It's a 5 step process.

Step #1: Pause (both of you). Bring your attention to this very moment. Don't think about your past or future. Take three deep breaths.

Step #2: Interlock your fingers. Hold each other's hands for 10 seconds. It is impossible to be mad if you are holding hands.

Step #3: Embrace your loved one in a heart-to-heart hug.

Step #4: Close your eyes, breathe deeply together, and remember you are alive.

Step #5: Think about where you will be in 200 or 300 years. You will be gone and forgotten. After about 20 seconds, you will realize just how precious it is to be alive and that your loved one is still there. How life is too short to choose anger over love.

If you try these few steps when you're having a fight with your lover or not having a good day, it will instead be filled with fun, accomplishment, and love. Granted, I probably wouldn't try these steps with strangers who are yelling at me. I'd stick with A, B, and C, listening, smiling, and trying to help them resolve the issues they are struggling with.

Do You Judge?

Why do people judge? Do you judge to make yourself feel better? In the Bible, it says we are not allowed to judge in several places, so why do we? I never was one who judged people harshly, but I admit that I did judge. As I got older, or as I like to look at aging, as I got wiser, I asked myself, "WHY JUDGE?" Because I'm far from perfect, and I've done things that even I would have judged myself. We are all human, so we all make mistakes. We all have minds of our own. So knowing this, I ask again, why do we judge one another? I want you to truly ponder this for a moment. It's just me, a book with words written by someone you will probably never meet, and you, the reader. No one else is around, so let your guard down, and truly think about how you treat others. Do you look at someone who is dressed a certain way and get that "OMG" thought? Do you wonder why she would leave the house looking like that? OK, politics—oh, how I dislike how violent people feel they have to get over political views. Just because you find out your neighbor or friend likes the opposing candidate, seriously, why on this Earth would you judge him or her for having a different opinion? If you can be civil and want to discuss why you both like your candidates, that makes sense, but when you disagree with why he or she likes that person and get the urge to fight back, you need to STOP, THINK, and KEEP your negative, judgmental thoughts to yourself and be thankful you are allowed and able to have different opinions and beliefs from those of your neighbor, friend, coworker, or family member.

Here's another example that happens a lot. Are you a parent? If so, this applies to you. Have you ever looked at another parent and watched how that person interact with his or her child and said, "I WOULD NEVER DO THAT"? It's OK to say that TO YOURSELF or even your spouse. I mean, you and your spouse should be one when it comes to marriage and parenting. But after you have that thought of "I WOULD NEVER DO THAT," do you judge that parent to be a lesser parent than you are? If you do—STOP! You don't know why that parent is parenting the way he or she is. Here is a prime example. Before my husband and I had kids, I'd see parents out there with leashes on their kids. I wondered why in the world they would do that to a child. Even after I had my daughter, I just couldn't understand why. Then my second child—my first son—came into our life. OH, MY, as sweet and lovable as this child was and is, he never understood staying still. When I went into parking lots with him, I ALWAYS had to hold onto him for dear life. When my daughter was a toddler, I taught her the rule of placing her hand on the door of the car 'til Mommy unlocks it, and there she stood. That did not work with my second child. The second I'd let go of him, he'd run. It was never to run away—it was just his brain telling him to go explore. I never let anyone, family included, watch my son unless it was in my home because I knew how fast he was. We use to frequent Disney a lot when we just had two kids. Guess what? I didn't want to have to relegate my son to being carried or have to hang onto him for dear life by the wrist or hand while we were there. I wanted him to have his freedom. So I did it. I became ONE OF THOSE PARENTS. I bought him a backpack with a leash. And you know what? My son was SO PROUD that he didn't have to hold our hands all the time, and he knew he was on a leash because he would ask my husband and me to take turns holding the other end. Oh, and guess what happened there? I got the looks, and I overheard the comments, and as much as I didn't like hearing those whispers or feeling those glares, I knew I was being the best parent I could by allowing my son to enjoy a day at Disney with his five-foot freedom while keeping him safe. To prove my theory, it cleared out at night, and all the crowds were gone, so I took off the backpack. Do you know what happened ONE SECOND LATER? He was off running as fast as he could like a little Forrest Gump. Needless to say, the park was empty, so we could see him, and my husband and I caught up to him, but that's just how he was 'til he turned about five or six.

Since then, I had another son, and I didn't have the issues with him that I did with my first son, which proves that everyone on this Earth is different, and what works for one person may not work for another.

We truly have no business judging one another unless we are 100% identical to the people we are judging and everything surrounding us is the same, which will never be the case.

Humans often assume that the natural world is run in a model similar to human communities. People recognize that we as humans are able to create order by creating laws and by establishing means of control. This humanlike viewpoint is a product of the natural pride that human beings take their ability to put meaning into this world. It is a profound acceptance of the fact that human beings are the actual source of values and any higher set of values that might be placed above the average human. They may attempt humiliation on the person and or encouraging guilt. In short, people who judge normally feel there is simply no other way the deed can be done. This is where we as human need to open our minds of understanding to the world, that there just never is a same scenario. All of our brains think differently and that this is a good thing.

Have you ever been judged? Think about it. Has anyone ever given you that look or whispered something behind your back or verbally attacked you about the way you should be doing something? Now think about how that made you feel. Did you enjoy it—the shame, the anger, the stomachache? If you answered "no," then what gives you the right to make someone else feel that way? I know I would have much rather not had those glares and comments when I was at Disney with my family because as you see, I still remember them, they're permanently part of my memories that I experienced from that vacation.

Your new goal now is to start tomorrow—and even better, today—to go out and not judge another you encounter. Instead, support, encourage, and smile at people. I'm not at all asking you to agree with everyone, but you can also be the bigger person by STOPing, THINKing, and KEEPing your negative thoughts to yourself. Think about WHY you are having those negative thoughts. Trust me, I don't always agree with certain things people do in their lives, but I don't judge them—those are their lives, and I am blessed to be able to do what I want in mine.

My husband and I have been landlords for several years, and we have met a lot of families along the way. So before you judge people about why they got rid of their pets, how they could give up their children, why they left their spouses, or why they committed crimes, just STOP and THINK --- does their situation have anything to do with YOU? Next, try to put yourself in their shoes. Maybe they had to rehome their pets because they got sick and were unable to care for them anymore. Maybe they lost their jobs, and money was so tight that it was either starve their pets or give them to happy homes. We have had several dogs over the years, and we've rescued hundreds more and rehomed them. I was in a situation where I had to rehome one of my fur babies, and I truly didn't want to, but I knew it was the best for the dog and my kids. I don't know why our dog did this, but when my second child was a toddler, this dog always looked at him as a toy. We tried all types of training to get her to stop this behavior, and she was fine with anyone other than my toddler. We truly think she thought he was part of her pack because he was so small. When I was pregnant with our third child, she got hold with her teeth of my oldest son's ear and pierced it, and it wouldn't stop bleeding. Although it broke our hearts to rehome her, I know we did what was best for everyone. She went into a home with no kids and they had another dog who was the same breed as she was. If we had kept her, she would have continued to hurt my son, and we feared that she would have attacked our newborn; in a way where she would think she was only playing. WE did what we thought was best for all of us, she went to a home where she would never be put into a situation where she could have done bad things, and my boys are healthy kids with no fear of dogs.

I'm sure there are good reasons people decide to rehome their children. I mean, how could they do it, right? I have three kids, and even though there are days I'd love to send them away, I would never rehome them. My life is them. Well, I was one of those kids who got rehomed. There're many stories out there about why I got rehomed when I was three, but some of my loved ones have gone to heaven and can't confirm or deny those stories, and really, it's life, and THAT'S Okay. No matter why my parents—who were teenagers when they had me—did it, and no matter why they separated, and no matter why I went from home to home between family and friends, it happened. I was that child everyone felt sorry for. The child of the parents who people judged for having me, for getting rid of me, for not always being there for me. It's life, and THAT'S Okay. I would not be the person and parent I am today if it weren't for everything that happened in my upbringing or all the love, care, and attention I got from the people who helped shape who I am today. I don't judge my family for doing what they did. It's what they all thought was best for me. They did what they thought was right.

I know so many people who say, "Oh, I would never do that!" But is your life exactly like theirs? Is your bank account, your family situation, your health, your support system the SAME as theirs? Because if not, you can't truly know what you would do in THEIR situation.

Social media is truly a 50/50 mix of good and bad. If you know how to use it, it can be the most amazing thing out there. But people also use it for judging, bullying, and thinking they are all that, but behind their computer is just them sitting there—and who are they really? What insecurities do they have to make them be the way they are?

I befriended a few homeless people over the past year, and one of them truly had NO ONE. His family wrote him off. He had no home, and he had medical issues but no insurance to help him get his medicine, and no doctors in the area were taking new patients like him (he did try to be seen). Due to his medical issues, he couldn't work. Sadly, I have no idea where he went; one day, he was JUST GONE. I'm praying that somehow, he found help and got off the street. But sadly, it could have gone the other way. Have you ever judged a homeless person on the side of the road? "Get a job bum?" I know when I was younger, I have had those thoughts of why don't they just get a job. Sometimes we get to a point in life where we fall and sometimes, we fall and get to the point its so hard to get up on our own. A person who is living on the street who were to walk into say a fast food restaurant and ask for a job, more than likely will be turned away because of their appearance and smell. If you are going to work with food you have to have good hygiene to keep everyone safe. Say they got a job, but still no place to shower and it would have to be in walking distance from where they were sleeping. Some times in life we need that extra boost to get us going in the right direction. Money in our account, a car, a place to stay with water and electric, and food and clothes. Sometimes a homeless person has had that extra boost from family and friends and the person failed to succeed with their boost. Some struggle more than others in life. It doesn't mean you should judge them. Instead just be there as a friend. If you financially helped them and watched them fail just still be there as a friend and continue to let them know they are loved. No one should ever feel like they are garbage.

Here is some more food for thought before I end this chapter. What if you are a judgmental person, and you constantly put people down, but you are also a parent, aunt or uncle, grandparent, or even a sibling to a young child. Children are always watching and listening to your every word and action.

Here's an example of me, the parent watching a show on Netflix—the last episode of that season. I so badly wanted to know how it ended. My household was sound asleep except my four-year-old and I. But he wanted to play with his Christmas gift. So, he played behind the couch not watching the TV. Well, the guy in the show said the F word, and what did I hear from behind my couch but, "F*&$!" I spun around so fast and tried explaining how that was a bad word. "What, F*&$, Mom?" my son asked. "Yes, we don't say that word," I said. My four-year-old again let out the F word, and I again explained that we DO NOT SAY THAT WORD! He listened, and thankfully, we haven't heard him say it again, but this takes me back to my point: guess who is always listening? What is the young child in your life learning from you? So, if you are a person who makes unnecessary comments or judges, your child is probably making those same comments, judging other kids he or she knows, and basically being a bully to his or her peers. Maybe the children being bullied feel they can't handle being judged and teased, so they take their own lives. This last year I read about how eight-, nine-, and ten-year-olds are TAKING THEIR OWN LIVES because they are being picked on and JUDGED by kids in their schools. EIGHT-, NINE-, AND TEN-YEAR-OLDS— WHAT IS THAT SAYING ABOUT US AS ADULTS and ROLE MODELS? We are failing our future.

Let's change the way life works. Let's not judge each other but rather help one another and know it is OK not to agree with each other's thoughts while still respecting each other's beliefs.

Judgment Day

Do you ever feel you must have something, or that something must be done a certain way? The next time you feel this way, ask yourself why. Is it for selfish reasons? Sometimes, being selfish is OK.

I pray every night for God to watch over my kids and protect them because I selfishly want them in my life. I want to watch them grow up into beautiful adults and make me some grandbabies who I can spoil and let them do all the things I wouldn't allow my kids and then send them home.

I am no saint. There are times I see things or read about disturbing events that happened, such as a story about a family where a mother and father chained their 13 children to their beds—and seven of those children were adults. Trust me, I could sit here and judge those parents for what they did. I mean, WHY—HOW!? But instead, I refocus what may have been judgment to thinking about those 13 individuals, and I'm saddened because they have endured such sheltered, tortured lives without safe love. And I pray that they can learn to love life and trust others the way parents should teach their children before they become adults and go into this world to be our future.

Judgmental thoughts come to every person's head. It's OK—it's going to happen. The important thoughts are what come out of our mouths or what we type online. It's kind of like writing a paper. You have your rough draft, your thoughts, and your topic. But you don't hand that in for your finished report. You need to write it out, re-read it, correct it, and then submit it.

That's what we need to do with our judgmental thoughts and feelings. Take that situation about the family with children chained to beds. These are some comments people made on social media about them:

> "NO TRIAL REQUIRED. SHOOT THEM IN THE BACK YARD."
> "SOMEONE NEEDS TO PUT A BULLET IN THEIR HEADS. SAVE THE TAX PAYERS SOME MONEY."
> "THEY NEED TO BE HUNG!!!"
> "ANYONE WITH A HAIRCUT LIKE HIM IS GUILTY."
> "DEMON POSSESSED. WHO TOLD THE MALE LUNATIC THE HAIR STYLE WORKED FOR HIM???"
> "THE WAY THESE TWO CREEPERS LOOK, NO DOUBT THEY WERE UP TO NO GOOD."
> "FEED THEM INTO A WOODCHIPPER, FEET FIRST."

You can probably guess there are thousands of other judgmental comments out there on social media. I jotted down the first seven I read. Having a judgmental thought is OK—again, it's what we do with that thought that matters.

Let's take the first one. The person right away thinks no trial is needed—let's just kill them. Let's take that angry thought and the fact that we judged these parents and made the call to end their lives. Now let's think deeper. Why were the parents doing this to their children? What happened to them? Did this happen to them as children first? Then shouldn't we feel bad that they had to go through the same ordeal and not understand what was normal? Now let's think about their children. Even though their parents were horrible role models, we instantly think that the kids have to hate them, right? Well, think about it. This was the only life they knew. The only parents they knew. I'm sure some of them—if not all of them—loved their parents in some way. It's got to be so confusing to each of them. Now we have taken them away from their mom and dad, and even though this is a good thing, some of the children may be struggling because their entire lives are changing. The kids are being separated, and they can no longer see or talk to their mom and dad. We will never know how these kids are feeling or will feel for the rest of their lives. But we as people can change our way of thinking about what is going on here. Instead of talking about different ways to kill their parents, let's look at how we can say positive words to the victims. How we are so sorry they were raised in the world the way they were because there really is so much good in this world. Let's pray that they can learn to love without punishment, learn to trust someone else to care for them. Let's pray that the state can keep these children together and not tear them apart. Let us hope we can find out why they were treated the way they were treated and learn how to see signs of this happening in other homes.

I was watching something on TV the other day after I wrote the above part of this chapter. It showed an image of a father beating a child, and the man on the show was asking another person whether the father should be judged. Then it showed another picture of a little boy being beaten by his father, and the person was asked whether that child should be the judge. The man replied, "No child should ever be judge," and I knew where they were going with this. That second child who was being beaten grew up and became a father, and he was the father beating the first child. Should he have remembered how his father made him feel when he was a kid and how he wanted to be treated so he could treat his own kin better? Absolutely. Sometimes, in life, things aren't as easy as they seem. Without the strength and support from family, friends, and even God, it's hard to change our ways from what was taught to us in childhood. This is one reason I am writing this book. I don't have all the answers, and some of my answers may not work for your life because I don't live your life. But I can teach you what I have learned and have seen and what has worked for me.

When my daddy drank, he would become violent. He knew just how to unbuckle that belt and with one flick of the wrist, pull it completely off his waist and whip it onto my backside. Conversely, my daddy loved me more than life itself when I was little. I was his baby girl, and he did all he could for me with the tools that were handed to him. I can't tell you exactly everything that went on in my dad's childhood because I wasn't there. What I can tell you is that he struggled greatly with learning in school. He was a wild boy, and my grandma's answer to his wildness was to tie him to a tree like a dog so he wouldn't run off. This is where my dad learned to love climbing trees. My grandma had five kids, and back then, there weren't a lot of helpful books or Google, and kids were all supposed to be the same or get labeled as problem children. My dad wasn't normal or the "cookie cutter" kid. He was a wild boy who always dreamed of true love and wanted to be loved by a girl. He could barely read, which made him feel dumb and less of a person. He grew up drinking to make him feel better, even if just for a moment. He was hot-headed and got into many bar fights and picked up so many ladies in hope of finding the ONE or feeling special. My middle son struggles with speech and reading, and I see a lot of my dad in him. I often look at my son and feel sad for my dad because his struggles were probably just like my son's, and sadly, the answer for him at that time was to tie him to a tree and just keep passing him through school with no one taking time to stop and help him. I am constantly working with my son and taking him to sessions with different therapists. He will succeed in life, and he will be confident knowing that he can learn and what he doesn't know he needs to continue to work hard at. I'm not going to allow him to just settle with the excuse that he struggles with skills that most of us find easy and not try his hardest to succeed in life. My son has two parents who love and adore him and are being hands on parents to him. We aren't going to be lazy and just tie him to a tree and let society raise our child. Now don't get me wrong. I loved her my grandma—my father's mom—to death, and if I had to compare myself to one person in the family, it would be her, to an extent, of course. She was free spirited, outgoing, dressed the way she wanted too, didn't let people put her down and was always willing to keep on learning. Those are traits I took from her. I'm putting this out here to show how easy it is to judge people without really knowing the truth in their lives. Every day, we are all struggling.

It's what we do with those struggles that matters. Do we let those struggles consume us and give up? Do we tie our children who struggle to a tree (or put them in a corner, or sit them in front of a TV) so we don't have to deal with them, or do we think about our future and the greater picture?

The hardest part of life is understanding why things happen. But the best part is learning why and not letting it hold you back but rather letting it build you into a stronger, wiser person.

Why Do We Do What We Do?

Have you ever asked yourself, "Why did I do that?" or, "Why did someone else do that?" When you're questioning yourself, you're teaching yourself. Deep down, have you felt that behavior is probably something you don't want to, or shouldn't, do again. So in asking yourself why you did it, you're learning and telling yourself not to do it again. We all make mistakes. Mistakes are OK and part of learning to grow into the people we are to become. The key with doing something wrong is to learn from it, to better yourself from not doing it again.

A friend and I were talking the other day about one of her friends who had cut her out of her life over a guy. Needless to say, the guy is now out of the picture, and they are trying to work on their friendship. This girl has kids from a former relationship, and she got involved and stayed with a man who beat her and controlled her. Why do we act senselessly at times? Why did this girl who has kids stay with that man? The very first time she got hurt, she should have taken her kids away from him and never seen him again. I understand there are times when you feel stuck and have no one to turn to, but this is where you need to be strong and do all you can to protect your children. You can't be afraid to have a happy life. You just have to make it happen. When you become a parent, your number-one job in life should be about protecting and teaching your kids so they can grow up to be better people than you are. My friend's friend, her way out was when he tried stabbing her with a knife and got arrested.

    Another friend of mine has struggled for several years wondering why she stayed with her ex-husband for so long. Why didn't she see the way he was treating her? Why didn't she realize she deserved better? Why did she even say, "I do?" She said, "Why did I not see the signs the universe was giving me not to do it?!" Then she said the magic words: "I learned never to think so little of myself that I need someone in my life." That's the answer right there. That was what she was to learn. We all make mistakes. We all want the best lives for our kids. It will hurt to watch them put themselves into situations we know aren't right for them. But we all have been in bad situations. We all should have learned from them, and if we didn't, then we need to stop and think, why did they happen? How can I make sure they never happen again? In life, sometimes, we need to be knocked off our high horses to realize life isn't always rainbows and butterflies, so we can learn to appreciate all the triumphs we do have and receive from life. I reminded my friend that even though she married the wrong guy for her, they made two amazing kids who are supposed to be here on Earth with her to make her an amazing mom. She also met this great man whom she probably wouldn't have otherwise if her ex-husband hadn't taken those years of her life. She probably would have met someone else. She probably wouldn't cherish how sweet her man is as much either. There is always a reason why stupid things are done in our lives. It's what we take from those stupid moments or chapters that matters.

I remember when I was a young teenager, I went out with a friend on his sister's boat with her husband. The sister and her husband started to argue, and the fight ended up in the bottom of the boat, where he grabbed a knife and pointed it at her. My friend stepped between them right away. In turn, I did the same thing. I stood with an angry guy holding the knife inches from my chest. I can still remember him questioning me, asking, "Do you really think I won't just go through you to get to her?" I can't recall my response—just looking him in the eyes and him putting the knife down and walking away. I had forgotten that story 'til the other day, when I was thinking about my friend's friend whose ex-boyfriend went to jail for trying to stab her with a knife.

Why did I, a 16-year-old, put myself in danger for someone I had just met a day or two earlier? I'd do the same thing again. But what if we hadn't been so lucky and the outcome had been different? My husband and I would have never met. My children wouldn't be here. I wouldn't be sitting here, writing this book. Sometimes, we have to trust our hearts and guts and do what is right at that moment. Sometimes, we need to protect ourselves and our children and stay away from certain people so certain things don't happen. The things we do and why we do them are stepping stones for us to learn how to become better people.

What is something you did this year that you questioned?

Jot it down:

Next jot down the outcome:

Now jot down the pros and cons:
Pros:

Cons:

Now looking back at what you wrote down, ask what you learned from this experience. Now let's review. What were the pros of what you did?

Here is a quote from one of my favorite authors and motivational speakers:

> *The secret of success is learning how to use pain and pleasure instead of having pain and pleasure use you. If you do that, you're in control of your life. If you don't, life controls you.*
> — *Tony Robbins*

No matter our past mistakes, we are always in control of our lives. Learn and better yourself from these mistakes to make them worth it.

It's one of the reasons we learn history in school: they want you to learn from the mistakes of the past so you don't repeat them.

Here's some important history facts you may or may not remember learning in school. Do you remember learning about when the National Air and Space Administration (NASA) used the metric system while Lockheed Martin used the imperial system when they built a satellite, resulting in a $125 million loss, the history mistakes are documented so we don't repeat and make the same mistakes again.

Do you remember in 1978, faulty equipment caused a nuclear meltdown at Three Mile Island, costing $836.9 million in repairs and clean-up.

Or how the failure to fix faulty equipment on the Challenger caused it to explode at liftoff, killing everyone on board and costing $5.5 billion in 1986.

Whether you remember these incidents or not, you can learn from them because they were all mistakes that shouldn't have happened, and we document them to remind us not to make them again. Your life is your very own history book. Learn from it.

Why Is the Past Hard to Let Go?

Do you ever catch yourself reflecting on how things were in your past? Have you ever wished you could just GO BACK and relive a moment you experienced?

There are times when I start to miss certain people who use to be in my life but are no longer there. Some have died, but others are still alive. I had one friend, who we will call Carter, who meant so much to me that it literally broke my heart to let this friend go, and I struggled with that for several years and still do a little today. But while I'm writing this book, I'm reflecting and trying to open my mind as much as I possibly can. I mean, I'm sure this person isn't missing me nearly as I am missing Carter. So why do I struggle with letting go? I've had several friends come and go, and sadly, I probably couldn't tell you the names of half of them or even recognize them. That doesn't mean they weren't friends and that I didn't enjoyed them. It just means my brain has moved on to the next phase in my life. But then, there're others who are hard to let go because they meant so much to me. I trusted them with everything or almost everything. I put in my time to be friends with them. I hoped the friendship would never end. Then it just does, sometimes for no real reason. Sometimes for a real reason, but why does that mean it's over? Sometimes, you know you shouldn't stay friends and see each other. You reflect on all the good times you had. But why? Why is it so hard to let go? When you think about these friends or people in your life who are no longer there, and you think about all the fun times you had and wish you could relive them, why? Maybe it's even something you used to do that made you a different person than you are today.

When are you thinking these thoughts? Is it when you are enjoying time with your current friends and loved ones, or you are feeling down or stressed at your current situation, or you just need a break from your everyday life? Do you find yourself thinking of happier times, whether it be doing something or being with someone?

After several years of reflecting about Carter, I realized the reason I had such a hard time letting go was because Carter was the first person with whom I got to be myself and have no secrets. This person taught me a lot about growing up and the real world. This friend believed in me when I most needed it and helped shape who I am. I noticed over the last few months or years that I haven't reflected on this person as much. As the days go by and I grow older, I have learned that it is okay to let go and not always have the answers to everything in life, and I continue to learn about the things in life that I can have and practice being even more open-minded.

When my husband and I argued, the kids stressed me out, life got hectic, or I was just having a bad spell, looking back at this person was like a kid going to a candy store. It was a reflection of me before bills, me before marriage, me before adult situations, me before kids. It didn't truly mean I wanted to leave my current life, but reflecting on my past was my escape from reality. Over the years, the way I looked at my past changed. I went from doing it constantly before I met my husband to occasionally afterward. When I was a child, I would reflect on memories of my parents and me living together, and I'd hope and wish we could go back to that.

Looking back at who we were and where we came from is always OK. But if we are hoping and wishing we could just jump back in time, and we spend all our time reliving our past, we need to ask ourselves, "WHY?" Reflecting on the past and reliving those memories in your head isn't real life, as much as you want it to be. So again, I ask, "Why are you stuck in the past? What do you want to change in your life that is making you feel that the past is the best place for you? Are you truly happy?" As hard as it is, we can't just stop life and stay in the past. We have to take a deep breath and look at what is right in front of us, what is ahead of us. Our future is up to us. We can choose to live in the past or look ahead and enjoy everything that you already have and everything that is at arm's reach in your future. The people beside you—the ones who are supporting you and the amazing person you are every day. Learn to let go of the past. Learn how to treasure what you learned from the past, but keep looking ahead and around you now.

Finding Out

I recently found out a dear friend of mine had passed away four months ago. She wasn't on social media much. I've known her for 34 years, and she was like family to me, like a mother or aunt kind of role model. She was my third-grade teacher. We always stayed in touch over my entire life because she meant so much to me and was so caring. My parents were teenagers when they had me. The marriage failed, and I was kind of bounced from one home to another. I was raised in the home of my aunt and uncle for most of my childhood. That is when I started elementary school. I had some teachers who would sympathize with my situation. I had a lot of adults in and out of my life, and they all wanted to be in charge of me, which meant I was going to several homes per week. Then I also had teachers who were cruel and would smack me in the head daily, just because they didn't like me, I guess. I mean, a six-year-old child who only wants to please everyone is EVIL. But when I turned seven, I met this amazing lady who not only understood my situation but was an outstanding teacher. I learned more in her third-grade classroom than I did in any other grade. This beautiful lady made teaching fun. No matter what subject it was, it came to life, and it was exciting. It was in her class I learned my love for writing and wanted to write books when I was older. It was her who influenced me to want to become a teacher—not a teacher who taught to a test, but one who taught so ALL students could learn. The year I had her, she had a young baby son at home, and I would ask her how he was doing every day. She would tell me about the new milestones he had conquered with a sparkle in her eye.

During my first year in college, I wrote my paper about this teacher and how she had inspired me to become a teacher too, and though I never became a teacher in a school system, I did become one to my beloved children. I have been so blessed to be able to homeschool them. And as you see by reading my words, I am writing a book for everyone to read and hopefully cherish. And last but not least, she showed me how a mother could love her child so dearly. I didn't have that with my mother. Our bond was strained. I didn't want that for my kids. I wanted to have that look of love in my eyes when I spoke of them—not the look in my mother's eyes that said they are a burden.

I am hurt that my third-grade teacher, my role model, my friend is gone. I am sad she is gone. I'm mad I didn't reach out to her more than I did because she did mean so much to me. But in the end, we need to look back at what we had with our departed loved ones and cherish, laugh about, cry about, and share with others the memories we had. We need to keep them alive in our hearts.

I sometimes go to my email and type in her name, and her email address pulls up, and I think, "She's still around, she's still with us because there her name is pulling up on my phone. The news of her being gone must be untrue." Then reality hits, and I know deep down she is gone. But that's when you must reflect on all the wonderful memories that you have of your loved one and think of them with a smile on your face instead of a tear in your eye.

A local singer, here where I live, passed away while my husband and I were on vacation. It was the first time we had taken a vacation without kids in 14 years. I had decided to take time off from social media, besides calls and texts to our kiddos and using the phone for pictures and looking up stuff to do in the area. My husband played on his phone for about five-to-ten minutes each day, but he also stayed off for the most part. The one time he was on, he told me a local singer had passed from cancer. I was heartbroken to hear this news. I knew he had cancer, and I thought he'd beaten it. My middle son had a big connection with him, and we met him on a few occasions and always listened to his music. Five years later, the song that made my son fall in love with him is still his favorite song. When my mother and kids picked up my husband and me from the airport, we started the van, and I heard his voice because the kids had been listening to him on the way. I had to tell them the news, and they all were shocked and saddened—even my mom. She went on to say how my kids had just introduced her to his music and told her all about him, as she lived out of state. Even though he wasn't a close friend, he meant something to us. Every time I hear of another person who's dear to us dying from cancer, it breaks me down a little bit more, and I think of everyone who's lost the battle to cancer and everyone who's beaten it. Then I fear for the ones who have beaten it because what if it returns? I don't want to lose them too. Then I fear getting cancer myself. What would I do? How would I treat myself?

When I was 13–15, I was introduced to cancer. I had heard from my grandma—my father's mother—years earlier that she'd had breast cancer, but she'd had surgery to remove it, and that was that. When I turned 13, though, my other grandma—my mother's mom—was diagnosed with ovarian cancer. This was the first time I'd seen cancer in its true form. I remember heading to the bathroom at my grandparents' place and seeing my grandma's full set of hair on the dining room table. I was stunned and confused. There weren't computers with internet back when I was 13, and I was uneducated. I remember feeling scared, I felt like who is this woman, how can she just rip off her hair like so? What else could she rip off? What else was fake? I just froze, looking at her wig sitting there on the table, trying to process why she had fake hair and why I had never noticed. "How sick was she really?" I wondered. "Why isn't anyone explaining to me the full story?"

I don't recall how old I was, but I remember visiting my grandma in the hospital with my mom. The nurse came in and said, "I need to give you a shot in the butt," and my grandma turned and looked at me and said, "Angela, go over there by the door and turn around." The nurse laughed and said to her, "We all have butts, and there's nothing different about them besides the size." I found that funny because my mother and her side of the family had always been reserved and private about medical issues and nudity. They were the total opposite of my father's side of the family.

I really wished I knew more about my grandma's sickness than I was told. I know they were only trying to protect me, but it only confused me more than anything. I couldn't understand why things were being done, like my grandma took me clothes shopping and told me I could buy anything I wanted. I never was a big shopper, but I found a pair of plaid pants that for some reason, I just fell in love with. But I remember looking at the price tag and seeing it was a price I would NEVER have paid for them, but my grandmother said, "Don't worry about it—I got it." The other thing I got that day was the only pair of MC Hammer pants I ever owned.

Around the same time, my grandmother sent my mom and me to a local water park to spend the day together. Shortly after that, my next memories are of her being bedridden at her home. I wasn't allowed to visit often, but I always wanted to visit and asked daily.

One day, I went for a visit, and grandma was up and out of bed. She wanted to cook me her famous grilled cheese with tomato. No one could ever make them like she could, and many had tried for me over the years. I remember telling her to rest, that it was OK, and that she didn't have to cook for me. She sternly said, "I'm going to make you this sandwich. I feel fine right now, and I really want to make this for you." It was my last happy moment I have of us together doing something we both loved, her cooking and me eating.

When my grandma passed, I felt I had to be strong for everyone else. I didn't cry about losing her 'til years later. I had several friends my age who'd lost their grandmas and to them it wasn't so emotional as my friends were younger when their much older grandparent had passed away. I mean, grandmas are normally old, and they die. It's just the way life goes, right? My grandma, however, was a young grandma—only 52—but it wasn't until I lost my father that I realized she'd been younger than he was when he passed, and that my mom had been younger than I was when she dealt with the loss of her mother.

Sitting here writing about these special people in my life, remembering them like they are right here, keeps them alive in my heart. Just because someone is physically gone in this world, it doesn't mean he or she is gone from you. Sit down and write your memories of your loved one—relive those favorite moments with that person. It may bring tears to your eyes, and you may be bawling like a baby, but that's OK. Just remember to smile and know the person is still here in your heart and mind, and because of that, he or she is not truly gone. Be open to watching for signs from him or her. Someone asked me if I had advice for people who have guilt about how they treated a person who they've lost. My advice would be to sit down and write the one who has passed a letter. Put all your guilt, all you pain, all your request for forgiveness in that letter. After you write that letter, I want you to open yourself to remembering all those happy moments you shared with that person. Reflect on only the positive memories you two shared and then I want you to burn that letter you wrote them. Let those feelings of guilt, anger, shamefulness leave you as you watch that paper burn. I want you to process that letter burning and how it is no longer there and notice how easily it was able to disappear, I want all those heartaches you hold to disappear with that letter that has gone, burned into ash, at that very moment. Don't look back at your pain only look forward to remembering your happy memories with your loved one who is resting in peace.

In 2016, my father passed away from cancer. It started in his lungs and finally spread throughout his body. It's amazing how when you encounter a death, so many people change, and a lot of them show their ugly sides. Some will think the person who is dying shouldn't have say. If their beliefs are different than the person who is sick, they try to overpower things. People start fighting over who is paying for what or not paying, they fight over the items the sick person has and they want, they try sneaky ways to get money from the person either while dying or after they have passed. I've heard stories where siblings have fought over a dying parents body of who that parent loved more. During death, you should come together and help and support one another, not be sneaky or ugly.

Ever since I was little, my dad would talk to me about death and what he wanted his death to be like. And no matter whether you agree or not, they were his wishes. We all have our thoughts about what we would like to happen to our body—our shell—when we pass. Some of us right away know we will be buried; maybe it's part of our religion. Maybe the thought of the ground and worms scares you, and you think of a mausoleum. Or maybe you want to be cremated because you feel your soul is out of your body and you don't need it anymore, so why take up space? No matter your belief or the reasoning behind it, you have an opinion. My dad's was for me to put him in a wooden box, throw him on a big bonfire, and celebrate his life. Well, I used to laugh when I was a kid and tell him if I did that, I would be thrown in jail. But when the time came when I needed to make sure his wishes were carried out as best they could be, legally, I was glad to find a funeral home that offered cremation with a viewing window (you really couldn't see anything but the machine they cremate people with). Behind the viewing window was a background that was composed of wooded trees with the sun shining through. It was perfect for what my dad's request had always been, and it was legal. I honored his wishes because it was what he wanted.

When my dad got really sick, he no longer lived in the same state as me. He asked me to bring my camera and take as many pictures as possible of him. Being a photographer all my life, of course brought my camera. However, I didn't realize how in-depth he wanted the photos to be until he passed, when my dad's baby sister who is also known as my aunt told me about this book he'd loved since he was a child: *Gramp*, by Mark Jury and Dan Jury.

It's a story about a three-year photographed documentary of an older gentleman's life as it deteriorates. There are pictures of when the man was young and holding his grandson, up to the end, when his grandson was carrying him around to bathe and change him.

However, I tastefully documented my dad's last few weeks of his life. And in doing, so I lost a lot of extended family. They couldn't understand how I could take pictures of my dad looking the way he did. They couldn't understand why I would document him and me playing a game of war cards, which we used to always play together. They couldn't understand how some of the family members and I videoed singing "Happy Birthday" to him with a cake and party hat we'd made for him and how we'd laughed with joy, all while he was unresponsive. We did it because he'd asked me to document him leaving. And although we were all sad and hurting, we were also celebrating his life. The family members and friends would come to visit for weeks, and we would all share the part of Randy we knew. Some of our recollections combined to complete full stories we each hadn't fully known. We didn't want to hold my dad back from passing by crying at his bedside. We knew there would be time for that after he passed. We wanted him to leave this place knowing he'd imprinted all of us.

When my dad left us, he didn't have much to his name. He'd said he come into this world with nothing, and he was going to leave this world with nothing. I asked him who he wanted to have the few things he did own. I wanted to make sure everything he wanted done would be done his way.

This is where it got ugly with a lot of people. They felt entitled to some of the things that were given to other people. My dad had reasons why he wanted his dear friend to have one of our family heirlooms, and I honored that even after his brother—my uncle—told me to keep it, and other people were mad because they didn't get it.

Whatever life you've lived, if you have a request on your departure—no matter what it is, as long as it is legal—why don't we honor it and make leaving Earth as easy as possible? It's not about Us, it's about Them.

Before my dad passed away, he always joked that he wasn't going to leave this world without a bang. At his memorial, we rented a pavilion on the water to eat outdoors—somewhere he would have liked to go. No storms were forecast that day. Well, as we were getting our food, a typhoon started. I mean, not only was the rain coming down, the wind was blowing it into the pavilion, making sure to soak everyone there. A male cardinal stood very close to the pavilion during the entire storm, not leaving to find somewhere dry. They say cardinals appear when angels are near. We all just laughed because we were there trying to eat our food, which was now soaking wet, and we told stories about Randy. After we ate, the sun came out, and it was as if the storm had never happened. We all agreed that was totally my Dad there leaving us with a BANG!

We left the motel the day after the memorial and piled into the car to head home. I was waiting in the car for my husband to check out, the song "Changes" by Ozzy Osbourne came on the radio. I couldn't even tell you the last time I heard that played on the radio. I knew it had to be my dad letting me know it was OK that I was leaving to go home back west and that he was going to heaven. The lyrics in that song just said it all.

I feel unhappy
I am so sad
I've lost the best friend
That I ever had
She is my baby
I love her so
But it's too late now
I've let her go
We're going through changes (ooh)
We're going through changes (ah, ah, ah)
We've shared the years
We've shared each day
I love you daddy

...

Days later, I started noticing I was looking at the clock at 2:22 p.m. and waking at 2:22 a.m., then at 1:11 p.m. and 1:11 a.m., and 3:33 p.m. and 3:33 a.m. I looked online to learn that these numbers are a special way for angels and spirit guides to get messages to you. I mean, I never in my life even thought about how cool it is that time can all be the same number, and shortly after my dad's passing, I constantly saw the time in the same triple numbers. My cell phone would literally be lying on a table, and when it was 1:11am or pm, 2:22, 3:33, 4:44, 5:55 it would just light up on it. I knew in my heart this was my dad.

One day, I was having a really bad morning and yelling at my kids. I just felt out of sorts, and as the morning went on, the madder I got. I started to see the triple numbers everywhere I looked. The gas price was $2.22, and license-plate numbers had 333 or 444. The clock on the radio showed the same three-digit time, 3:33 p.m., and to top it off, there a song came on the radio—"I Will Always Love You"—and it was written on the digital screen too. It was what I needed to hear just then to calm me down and refocus, and I knew it had to be my dad.

There are always signs out there for us. We just have to be open to seeing them. Thinking about our loved ones who passed, writing down memories of them, talking about them, and looking at photos of them will keep them alive in us and should give us comfort in our hearts, knowing they aren't gone forever.

∞ ∞ ∞

Dating

Your dating life. Have you ever regretted dating someone? Maybe you think, "I can't believe I wasted all those years with someone who treated me horribly." Don't! You need to change your way of thinking.

I dated this one guy before my husband for several years. I'm going to give him a fictional name so you can follow along easier. We'll call him "Bill" in this book. I'm not sure what drew me to Bill to say, "Hey, let's have a relationship," but something did. I still remember to this day, at the very beginning, him telling me I was going to end up hating him and leave him. Well, the leaving part did happen several years later, but the hating part didn't.

He was an adult, and I was still in my teen years when we started to date, so when he asked to help me out with getting credit cards and doing my banking, I didn't think twice about it. I mean, he was my boyfriend, and he cared about me, and he only wanted what was best for me and wanted to teach me, right?

I was wrong. This was the first "yes" I gave him for him to control me. I wasn't allowed to withdraw money without his permission even though it was mine. I was given a small allotment $10 or $20—to live off for the week for my lunches and gas money. Because I didn't have much money, it made me unable to visit my family or friends very often. At the time, I didn't fully realize he was trying to isolate me.

When Bill bought his first home (moving out of his parents' home), the controlling become worse. He'd wait 'til I got to his home from work for me to take off his shoes, and there were several other must-dos for me. It got to the point I realized this wasn't love, and he was never going to love me. He wanted me for show and basically to be his slave.

I'm not here to bash this person and not going to relive all the memories. But I will tell you, in the several years I was with him, and even though he made me wear clothes and makeup the way he wanted and put me down daily, I never lost ME. What I did lose or never learned to use was my confidence. That was hiding in me somewhere. But I knew what was happening wasn't right. One reason I didn't fight back too much was I loved his family. I didn't want to lose them. It's sad how when a breakup happens, you don't just separate from that one person—you honestly are separating from his family and friends too. That was hard for me to be OK with.

One day, I just had the confidence to make this separation happen. But because of the situation I was in, it couldn't just be a quick split. It was a six-month process. I was then 21, and I used that to my advantage. I wanted to be able to go out with friends once a week to the bar. He was over that scene because he was a little older than me and a homebody. After I got that one night a week where I was allowed to stay at my place and go out with friends, I worked on pretending to be stupid and asking him to teach me how to bank and pay bills myself. This was something I had already learned before ever becoming an adult, but I needed to get my life back, but also protecting myself in the process. He had everything of mine. I needed to get control of my finances that he had of mine before walking out that door.

Once all my personal investments were untied from him and under my control, the day came when I got the courage to break up with him. Of course, according to him, it wasn't my idea to break up with him—but it was all me. It was all me because I was losing myself being with him.

Maybe you recall how a few paragraphs ago, I said hating him didn't happen. Well, it honestly didn't. I learned a lot being with him. He wasn't always a bad person, but then again, that's how a lot of abusive relationships work. They treat you nicely to feel OK with how they treat you poorly. For me, like I said, I left him without hate toward him or even anger. I mean, I could have left him long ago, even if he told me I couldn't survive without him because part of me still didn't believe him. It was all me who stayed as long as I did. I needed to find me before I could end the abusive verbal relationship and stand strong to end that chapter of my life and move on to the next one.

The real reason why I didn't have anger toward Bill or hate him was because I learned from him all those years I spent with him. Some things were for the good. The bad I learned from him I used in my life to know HOW NOT TO TREAT SOMEONE.

I honestly believe that the reason my husband and I clicked so well was because we both were coming from not-so-good relationships. And being in a bad relationship teaches you how not to treat your current significant other and how to appreciate the little things he or she does for you even more.

If I had ended the relationship earlier or later than I did, I would never have met my husband or started to date him. He only lived in the same town as me for six months before his job moved him an hour and a half away.

I am a true believer that things in life happen for a reason, good and bad. How we look and learn from what happened is our true lesson in life. If you are the type of person who is always looking at the negative things in life and feeling the blues and feeling like you will never get ahead, then you are looking at life the wrong way. What's something bad that happened to you recently? Think about it. How could you turn that bad around and look at the positive in it?

Some examples: You got a flat tire on a day you were already late and had to be somewhere in 20 minutes. You could have looked at that flat tire and stressed that you were going to be late or may even have had to cancel. But was your tire flat because it saved you from being in a car accident? I can't tell you how many times in my life I came up minutes behind a wreck on days something odd like that has happened to me— something that made me drive later than I had planned.

Maybe you feel trapped in your life. Think about why. What do you need to stop feeling that way? No matter what it is, you have to just work hard toward the goal of being happy. I'm not saying you won't encounter a ton of roadblocks. If you do encounter them, it's to make you stronger so you can feel so much more accomplished at the end of your journey.

Maybe your childhood wasn't perfect. Learn from it. How did certain things that happened make you feel? Did you not like how you felt in that situation? Remember that feeling when you become a parent.

Understand how your children feel if they are put into the same situation, and be a better parent or role model so they don't have to carry that same pain or embarrassment.

I didn't date a lot of guys in my life. I'd been friends with most of them for a good while before getting into relationships with them. My second boyfriend was the first guy I truly loved. I mean, really loved. I'm also going to give him a fictional name. Let's call him "John." John was the one I dated with the biggest age gap between us, which is the real reason things didn't work out. I was still a teenager and still trying to figure out who I was going to be in life. He was the first guy to encourage me to be me, to find me, and to live my life for me. He set the bar high for my future hunt of my future husband. At that time, I would have never compared him to my dad, but looking back some 20-plus years later, he was a lot like my dad. He was hard-working, he loved to spend his money on women, he was a huge flirt, he made me laugh, and most of all, he made me feel safe. We dated off and on over a year, and even though I knew he wasn't the one I was going to spend the rest of my life with, he was my first true love. He gave me confidence as a teenager that I then started to lose again growing into an adult. After we ended our dating relationship we still kept in touch off and on. Our relationship over the next several years was platonic, but the flirtation never stopped. I always felt we were so connected in a way I truly could never explain. When I dated that controlling guy, Bill, I didn't speak to or see John, but when things with the controlling relationship got worse, I started hoping daily that John would come and rescue me from that relationship. There wasn't a day that went by that I didn't think about him. In reality, I feel John was the reason I put up with as much as I did because I knew there were good people out there. I knew my life didn't have to stay the way it was going. After Bill and I broke up, I reached out to John, and he responded and once again was in and out of my life in a platonic way.

We would talk to each other about life, friends, and current relationships for hours and hours on the phone.

I really, to this day, don't know how John truly felt about me. He dated a lot of girls in his time, just as my dad did. But I know he cared for me in some way to keep some type of relationship going. He didn't love me like I loved him; he was my first true love. By true love, I mean there is love, and you will feel that for many people in your life, but then there is true love—deep, deep, emotional, lasting feelings toward someone. That is what I had toward John. To my dying day, I will still love him, but in the way, I love a dear friend. His feelings toward me may not have been how my feelings toward him were. In life, situations like this happen often, and IT'S OKAY. It's how we handle and accept not having the same experience or feelings as the person who we just were with. During the time he and I spent together, I learned so much about myself. Who I needed to become. The type of husband I wanted in my life. He made me a better person without even knowing it. Even though our feelings weren't the same for each other, it doesn't matter. It's all about what we learn and take from the experiences in our lives to better ourselves for our futures.

I want to tell you about another experience I had with dating. This one was with some random guy who I knew nothing about. My friend and I waved to him through a window at a restaurant where we were eating. The next thing I knew, he was standing at my table asking for my number. I had just broken up with my first true love a few months prior, and I needed to get back out in the dating world, or so I thought. When he picked me up at my house, he honked the horn—he didn't even have the courtesy to get out of his car and come to my door. We left to go to dinner, and he didn't put his seatbelt on. I'm big with seatbelt safety, so that was strike two before we even left my driveway. I should have ended the date right there. When we got to the restaurant, he decided we should only order dessert. UGH! This guy was not for me. This date couldn't end soon enough. He finally took me home and dropped me off. I don't remember when he called me again, but my goodness, he would not stop calling me. He kept asking me out. All I was thinking was, "Were you not on the same date as me?" I told him my concerns about why I didn't want to go on another date with him, and he begged for a do-over. So, whatever. Because I am a nice person, I decided to try again. I mean, it couldn't go any worse, right? The next date he came to the door and picked me up. He put on his seatbelt while telling me, "I knew you were one of those types of people." I should have gotten out of his jeep right there as well. He asked me what I wanted to do but didn't listen to any of my suggestions. Instead, he decided to take me "parking" to make out. Like, making out with this guy was something I totally wanted to do, NOT! He wouldn't stop and pushed himself more and more onto me. Luckily, I had a pocketknife that was given to me by a friend. I never in my life would have thought I would have been in a position where I needed to protect myself like that. For most of my life growing up, I'd let people push me around until that moment—age 17—when I opened the blade to my knife and placed it on his neck and advised him to take me home and never to call me again. I debated putting this in here, but you know what, things like this happen every day—and things far worse. You need to always be able to protect yourself. Back in my young dating years, cell phones were not a popular thing, and on this date, I did not have one. Never let anyone put you in a situation you do not want to be in. If they do, say "no," and protect yourself, however, try staying calm so you are always in control. He took me home that night, and we never spoke again. I felt strong and in control of my life after standing up for myself. I may not have always made the best choices after this day, but it was a good learning experience.

It's funny writing about these past relationships because I don't ever speak about my ex-boyfriends to my husband. Well, besides my preschool boyfriend who I kissed on the playground. It's kind of a joke in our household. My father would always speak about his exes around his current girlfriends or wives, and I never understood why he did that. Even as a child, I cringed when he talked about an ex around a new partner. I mean, I understood the exception where if you have a child with someone, that person may be brought up from time to time. But why speak of a past relationship in comparison to the new person in your life? Anyway, my husband and I spoke about our past relationships in terms of what we felt we needed to tell each other in the first few weeks we were together, but after that, we just stopped talking about them. I think talking about your ex over and over again is a way to remember them. But why would you want to continue reliving memories of your exes—especially to your current love? Your current love should be your number-one focus in the relationship. For a healthy relationship, you should treat your partner like there is no other person who matters. Bringing up memories of your exes puts doubt in your spouse's or loved ones head.

Let me go off the topic for just a moment. One may ask well she's telling me not to talk about my exes around my partner, but yet here she is writing about her exes for all of us to read, including her husband. Firstly, my husband knows I'm writing this book and is aware of what is written here. Secondly, I wrote this in hopes to help someone else understand something they maybe going through, have gone through or protect them so they won't go through the same thing. My husband and I are in an amazing spot in our relationship. We both know that we love and support one another. I'm not comparing my exes to my husband. I am explaining some key points in my past relationships in hope to teach others to understand. Okay, back on topic now.

If you are someone in a relationship where it truly doesn't bother you, having your current love repletely talk about their exes, well then, good for you for having tough skin. None of us in this world are alike, and I give you my advice based on my experiences or the experiences I've seen around me. So I am admitting I am not perfect, and I am not you. And you may disagree with some of my words of advice. But that is the glory of life, the luxury of allowing each of us to have our own thoughts and feelings. If you are someone who has such thick skin that this TRULY doesn't bother you, then this advice isn't for you. However, to a lot of us out there, this and the other advice in this book will help you be a better person and succeed in life.

In a marriage, you should never have to be compared to someone else—especially to an ex. In a marriage, you should be able to be 100% you. But we'll talk marriage in another chapter.

Jealousy

Jealousy can be a very ugly thing. It's something that eats away at us. It causes anxiety, insecurity, and bitterness toward people.

There are many types of jealousy. There's only one that I like—the one when someone is like, "man, I want that too," but at the same time is happy you were able to get or enjoy it.

Do you know someone who gets things you really want? Maybe a person who gets to go on those vacations you really want to take too? Do you get that anger in your stomach because "that's not fair"? Do you maybe have evil feelings toward that person? Stop. Think why you are having those feelings. Is their life yours? In this scenario, you need to learn to love yourself and the life you have. If you aren't happy with your life, change it. Don't complain that you can't and don't use money as an excuse. You are living and breathing. You must realize that living and breathing is amazing and means something—the very most important something. Now, how you look at life and yourself after appreciating the fact that you are breathing and loving yourself is the next most important thing to do to help you not be jealous of what others have. In fact, when you see others happy, if you are in a good place with yourself and able to learn and understand how to be humble, you will be happy for others and appreciate the life you have for yourself. You will no longer be angry or have the anxiety of jealousy toward them.

People who don't get jealous—or at least not to the point where it doesn't bother them for a long time—avoid it because they surround themselves with trustworthy people, happy people, and humble people.

Now, have you ever thought you wanted something just because someone else can't have it so you can flaunt it in front of him or her. Or wanting something because you know someone else wants it for a sentimental value and that's the only reason you want it, well, that's not okay. If you feel this way, it's OK, but you need to ask yourself why. Then ask yourself whether that is mature reasoning. We cannot always help the thoughts that run through our head. But we can control their outcome. Controlling the outcome of our thoughts also helps train our brains not to be so jealous and greedy.

The way we are brought up doesn't dictate the way we will turn out. It's up to us to accept that we are in charge of our own lives. Only you can take action to better yourself. But that's the true secret that a lot of us are not told—even though we should be. You are in control of your life no matter what your past was like.

What are five things you own that you are proud you bought?
1.
2.
3.
4.
5.

What are five things in your life that you are proud you got as a gift (you may not still have this gift, but it made you proud to have when you did)?
1.
2.
3.
4.
5.

Who are five people who you are proud to have in your life?
1.
2.
3.
4.
5.

Now look at these 15 things and people you listed. That's a pretty nice list you have there, right? They all have special meaning to you. The next time you get jealous, stop and think of these 15 things and people, and realize how much you have or had in your life and how privileged you are. All of us have things in our lives to be grateful for, and when jealousy strikes, it means we aren't appreciating the 15 things or people listed above. Stop and maybe spend time with one of—or all of—the five people listed above, or dust off one of those 10 things and use it. Enjoy what you have, and you will see things in a different light.

Now what about jealousy in a relationship. You and your partner are together and another person comes into the picture and you become jealous of that person. STOP! Take a deep breath and ask yourself, why are you jealous? This feeling I know doesn't feel good, so why have it? What is causing you to be jealous of this other person? The biggest step is trying to figure out what the root of this pain is. Was trust broken? Was trust broken in a past relationship so you figure trust will be broken in all relationships? Do you feel you OWN this person and he or she shouldn't even talk to anyone except you? Finding out the root of the jealousy is the number one step. If trust was broken with this person in the past you need to sit down the two of you and talk about it. After you have talked about it, you need to let it go and start over fresh. If you can't forgive and forget then you will never be happy and this relationship would not be healthy for either of you. Now if you are feeling this way because in the past you were burnt then let the other know, explain why you feel this way, then shut that door behind you and move on with a start fresh. Now if you feel that person belongs to you, STOP! You are having the wrong image of a healthy relationship in your head. No one belongs to any one, period! Everyone is their own person and should be treated as such. You should be honored to be allow to spend time with this person and to have them want to spend time with you. So, if you feel this way think about how life would be without them in it. Think about what brought you two together. Think about how lucky you are that this person came into your life. Now start appreciating that person and know that you are the one that is lucky they are in your life. Learn to share and learn to be okay with that. And you, in turn, will have an amazing feeling of life, love and happiness.

∞ ∞ ∞

Marriage

So many people go into marriage with puppy-dog eyes and fairytales in their heads. I have been married for 18 years and have been with my husband for 20. I walked down that aisle to marry him without one second wondering whether I was making the right decision. I knew in my heart he was the one.

My dad had three failed marriages and many other failed relationships in between them. He dreamed of that perfect, happy, everyday fairytale of "happily ever after." The problem with that was he picked the wrong women, and he himself was wrong with those women. How did he have three failed marriages? How does anyone end up divorced? Well, I'm going to tell you what I have learned in my life. It all started back when I was 19. I had a friend tell me not to even think about marriage 'til I was 21. I thought, "What in the world is this girl thinking"? Well, now that I have lived way past my 21st birthday, I can explain this theory to you just like I explain it to my children. If you fall in love in your young teen years and say it's going to last forever, great. Marriage doesn't have to happen to make a relationship last—in fact, it only complicates things. So if you are under 21 and want to get married, date and plan your future together, but get married when you turn 22. By the time you are 22, you will be a full adult. You can drive your car anytime of the day or night, you can vote, and you can drink. You legally can do all the things that were once restricted from you. When you turn 21, you change. I'm not saying for bad or good. You just change because you have the freedom to do anything you want to, legally. I have learned that when you turn 21, not everyone wants to go to the bars. Some want to party like crazy, but others may not want to drink at all. But until you turn 21, you really don't know the type of person you or your partner will be. The person you are dating may be a few years older than you are and can't wait 'til you turn 21, and when you do, he or she may be over that scene of going out, so you may be trapped because you want to explore that scene. If you truly love someone, and you want to be married, and you are younger than 21, what's the real difference between being married right away and waiting a few years just dating and being engaged? Nothing, and besides, you get to continue to learn about each other and save more money for your wedding day. Once you are married and have made a commitment, you have let that person be part of you on paper. It is far easier to end a dating relationship then a marriage. Waiting a few extra years to confirm your love has stayed the same will be the best financial and emotional decision you will make. Even an unexpected pregnancy doesn't mean you have to get married, especially nowadays.

Let's talk about some important words you need to follow in a marriage.

#1. Honesty. I can't tell you how many times I have spoken with friends who tell me stories their spouses don't know about because they are lying to them. In a relationship, both parties must be honest with each other. If you are bothered by something and you don't tell your partner, then it will continue to fester in you. Your demeanor will change. You may not even be upset with your partner, but he or she may think you are because you are not being honest with each other. The negative energy that comes off someone who isn't being honest changes the people around you. You may not even be aware that others can pick up on it, and maybe you are good at hiding it from friends and family, but your partner—who is engaged in your well-being—will know. They will feel the rejection and feel smaller, and they may spend the next few hours or days trying to figure out what they did to you. It really hurts when you reject your partner and shut down on them, and they will eventually lose respect for you and do the same to you. This step sometimes takes a bit of work with yourself. Sometimes, it's just easier to shut down, but if you want your marriage to work and be healthy and happy, you must be honest with each other and talk to one another.

#2. No judgment. I'm a firm believer that none of us have the right to judge. We can have different opinions, but we shouldn't judge people. The number-one person you should never judge is your spouse. The two of you should be able to be yourselves around each other. If you can't be yourself around your partner, then you are not ready for marriage. The commitment of marriage should be for when two people become one. You two should be stronger because you have each other. No matter your thoughts or beliefs, you should respect each other and never judge each other. The first time you judge each other, a wall goes up, and honestly it puts your marriage into jeopardy.

#3. Trust. Do you trust the person you are with? Or are you someone who has to go through each others phones, emails, and social-media accounts? Sadly, it is very easy for people to cross that line with social media. However, it's up to you to believe in your relationship and yourself. A healthy, strong relationship has trust. You must not be jealous of each other. Jealousy is an ugly thing, and it will eat away at you. You both need to work together to make sure you are being faithful and trusting and believing in each another. Don't listen to outsiders unless you truly have a gut feeling. My husband would travel a lot for work, and he often traveled with female coworkers. I never had an issue with this because I trusted him and knew our relationship was OK. I recall people over the years of our marriage would make comments such as, "How do you know he's not with other girls there or going to strip clubs?" (not that there is anything wrong with going to a club, as long as it's not being hidden from your partner and you both consent to it), especially when he would travel to Vegas. I always replied, "Because I know my husband, and I trust him." The people who do this to you are normally people who don't know how to trust or have been hurt before or are just plain jealous of what you have. You have to shrug them off and believe in the commitment you made to each other on your wedding day: "I promise to be your *faithful* partner in sickness and in health, in good times and in bad, in happiness as well as in sadness." If the two of you don't trust each other, you must sit down together RIGHT NOW and explain why, and you must not judge each other but instead must listen and be honest and figure out how to create trust again in your marriage, or your marriage will fail. Which brings me to:

#4. Communication. Have you ever heard the saying "communication is key?" I will tell you that is 100% true. Not only in marriage—but especially in marriage.

These steps we are going over all go hand in hand, which is why it is so important that you do them all to succeed. If something is bothering you, be honest and communicate your feelings to your loved one. When you come home from work, ask how each other's days went. Talk about your future together. When you let the TV, your cell phone, the internet, or game systems get in the way of communication, it's easy to slip into a routine where there is just silence in your home and your relationship. Communicating online or through text is nice for a small dose of little things such as saying "I love you" by text or posting something cute, but it doesn't consist of the kind of communication I am speaking about. You must put everything away and look at each other and actually listen and engage in conversation. It took my youngest son at age four to make me realize we, as a family, had stopped talking. My husband and I were fine with our time together. I homeschooled the older two kids, so I spent all day talking with them. My youngest, however, was at preschool all day and would come home to eat dinner, and the five of us would sit around the TV and eat, and then pretty much get the kids ready for bed. My youngest told me we needed to start eating dinner at the dining room table with no TV. He was right. I felt like the worst parent, allowing my laziness get in the way of the five of us sitting down at the table and listening to each other's days. Communication is so important in every aspect of life, but it's more important to have with your spouse and kids.

I kind of mentioned this step with communication, but:

Step #5 isn't a word—it's an action. It's the small things that count. I'm not big on having flowers delivered a lot. I think there're so many other things in life you could use that money for. I am, however, not against flowers. I think giving flowers to a male or female shows love and appreciation. Yes, I have given my husband flowers before or plants. Not nearly as many times as he has given them to me, but the local stores normally carry flowers that run $5–$10 for something small but sweet. If you or your loved one is having a bad day, pick up some flowers on the way home to brighten both your days and your home. During your breaks at work, stop and send an "I love you" text, or ask, "How is your day, sweetie?" Text something you wouldn't say to anyone else. My husband and I have been together for 20 years now, and we text each other small "xoxo"-type texts every day. Every time I get an "I love you" or "How is my lady?" text throughout the day, it brings a smile to my face. Maybe your loved one has a favorite sweet—try to bring it home on a no-special-occasion day. Doing these small gestures really counts and will keep your love in the air.

So let's review all the things I went over for a happy, healthy marriage relationship.

A good piece of advice for marriage is waiting 'til after your 21st birthday, such as marrying after you turn 22.

> *Step 1 in marriage is to be honest with each other all the time.*
> *Step 2 in marriage is no judgment.*
> *Step 3 in marriage is trust each other 100%.*
> *Step 4 in marriage is communication.*
> *Step 5 in marriage is the small things count.*

Now, I'm not saying my way is law, or that if you don't go by what I say, then you will be doomed in your marriage. I am, however, saying that based on what I have learned and seen in other marriages and my own doing, these six steps will guarantee a happy marriage when two people really love one another. We all fight in marriage, but it's all about what we take from those fights that strengthens us and helps us succeed in our marriage.

About seven years into my marriage—which seems to be when most couples struggle—we stopped doing steps 1-5. It got to the point that we were both ready to throw in the towel, which is what I see with so many failed marriages. It's almost easier to just walk away, especially when you stop doing and then forget all about steps 1-5. You get to that point because you failed to do step 5, then step 4, and probably step 2 got failed next, and then step 1, so of course, step 3 was no longer happening. It can happen, and it did happen in my marriage. I will always remember the moment I threw in the towel and said we either needed to change our ways—the both of us—or end it today. Well, as you know, we changed our ways. We both did, and we first started with step 5 to fix the broken, once-solid relationship we had. Then we worked on steps 4, 1, and 2, and with that, step 3 just came back. I don't regret our almost failure because it made us have an even stronger marriage. Because we've experienced that horrible place where we once were, we now catch ourselves quickly if we are failing any of those steps. We stop and fix it before losing any more.

What steps are you missing in your relationship or do need to work on?

The song "Jolene" came on the radio, and as I was singing along and remembering listening to it over and over and over again on my dad's record player when I was a little girl, I listened to the words and thought about it more deeply. It is an old country song sung by several people over the years. Olivia Newton–John's was the version I used to listen to on the record player, and Dolly Parton's version was the one on the radio playing that day. But the song says,

*"Jolene, Jolene, Jolene, Jolene,
I'm begging of you, please don't take my man.
Jolene, Jolene, Jolene, Jolene,
Please don't take him, even though you can."*

I loved this song as a child and never thought anything was wrong with it.

When I listened to these words again, still loving the song because it reminded me of the times I spent with my dad, I thought how that's not a way to live, especially if you are married. You should never have to feel like someone may steal your spouse. If you do, your marriage needs some help. I know deep down I never have to worry about those Jolene's out there. If any girl wants to try to take my husband away from me, she will fail. And if for some reason, he fails and goes off, then that's on him, not Jolene. No one in a marriage should ever have to worry about whether Jolene will steal your man. For a happy, healthy marriage, you must commit to each other. Pine for each other. The moment you feel things shifting—and they will—stop and communicate with each other. Listen to each other. You both will have to give in to the needs of each other, and you both should have a partner who will give in to your needs. Marriage should be a 50/50 balance. Our needs are also constantly changing as we grow older. What we may have needed in our 20s isn't what we need in our 40s, 60s, or 80s.

I mention the word "balance" because it reminds me of a bracelet, I bought my husband. I've bought jewelry over the years for him, and he sometimes wears it here and there, but he never really committed to wearing any besides his wedding band and a cross necklace from our oldest son. He works in the office, so he normally dresses in professional clothes. I found an online club that sold these amazing inspirational reminder bracelets made of stretchy material that didn't look professional at all. But I got him this one with a yin yang and fish on one side that looked very manly, and if flip it over to wear it inside out, it reads "BALANCE." He wears it daily. In life, no matter the situation, you need balance. Balance for work, friends, school, family, and you. If you spend too much time in one spot, your balance will be off. In marriage, you have to balance the relationship among your wants, your partner's wants, your children, your bills, your fun activities, change in each other, and your sex life. My husband went to work one morning and forgot to put on his bracelet when he got out of the shower. My daughter found it later that day and brought it to me. He called me later saying he was having a horrible day at work—nothing was going right. I joked and said it's because he forgot his balance bracelet. He paused and said, "You know, ever since you got me that bracelet, it has reminded me how important balance is in your everyday life, and I was remembering that because I was wearing it to remind me. The first time I forget to put that bracelet back on, I had a horrible day." Now, the bracelet isn't what makes or breaks someone's day. But the fact that he started to rely on looking down at his wrist during a tough moment and seeing the word "BALANCE" refocused him to train his brain to stop, breathe, and do. We all will have a bad day when something will set us off, but how long we hold on to that anger is what counts.

Never going to bed mad is something we have practiced in our relationship. I can honestly say that we have been together over 20 years now, and I probably went to bed mad just a handful of times. And those times probably shouldn't have happened. I was probably just too tired to resolve the issue first, which isn't really a good enough excuse. I have never once sent my husband to the couch to sleep, and we have always kissed each other goodnight before bed.

Money

I know I've talked about money before off and on in this book, and I may repeat some important key facts, but sometimes, for some people, repetition is key.

What is one of the top reasons why married couples fight? Bingo, MONEY!

If we took money out of the relationship, that would eliminate 85% of common fights in most marriages where people don't communicate well or aren't on the same track with each other about how it should be spent or saved.

Even people in the happiest of relationships sometimes fight over money issues at least once a month. My husband and I are once-a-monthers—maybe even a couple times a month, depending on the time of year. I'm big with throwing birthday parties for our kids, and once a year, we have what we call a Halfoween party with a Halloween theme halfway through the year. He'd much rather I didn't spend the money for these parties, but at the end of each of them, he always tells me, "You did a good job, baby. Everyone had so much fun." We will not be on this Earth forever. Leaving your money to loved ones can help them financially, but the memories of what they did for you or with you will remain their entire lives. Memories are worth way more than a bundle of money left from a relative after he or she passes.

My dad always told me, in so many words, he was born into this world with not owning a thing, and he was going to leave this world not owning a thing. This came true for him. My dad was never taught how to handle his money. When he got paid on Friday, we would go to the finest restaurants and eat the biggest steaks. He'd buy the girl of the week jewelry just to impress her. But when Monday rolled around, he was counting his change to be able to buy gas for his truck. He was content with this lifestyle. I, however, watched the struggle he faced weekly, and I never wanted that for myself. One time, in my adulthood, my dad said, "I hope I taught you something that you use in your lifetime." I joked with him and replied, "Oh, yeah, you did, Dad. You taught me how NOT to handle my money." But he also taught me not to hold on to it so tight I couldn't enjoy life. I learned from him that I wanted the best of both worlds. I wanted to have money to spend on those things that meant something special to me or a loved one but not spend so much money that it left me poor. Balance is what I wanted.

When I first met my husband, we both weren't at the financially stable part of our lives. We didn't have each other yet to succeed in life to our fullest. I say "fullest," but I don't believe we have even met that because that would mean we have nothing more in life to strive for. You should always want to continue to better yourself.

My husband and I both met each other in our young 20s, and we both didn't have a lot to our names. He just didn't care about bills and money, and he literally would let the bills pile up and not pay them, which in turn gave him late fees and hurt his credit. Part of the reason wasn't even that he didn't have the money—it was because he kept himself so busy with work, he just didn't care. I, on the other hand, struggled paying my bills. I barely was making enough to get by, and that was it.

When I fell in love with my husband, I started to realize the importance of growing up and wanting to be successful in life. No one ever taught me how important managing your money was or why. No one ever taught that to my husband either. So we both started a relationship with debt and didn't know and understand the importance of credit scores. When we talked about marriage, I wanted us to clean our slates and start our marriage with only debt we incurred together, not in past relationships or on our own. I ended up needing help and went to a debt consolidator to help me clean up my past debt before my wedding day. That is one thing I would suggest to anyone looking to get married. When you marry someone, no matter how perfect that person is, he or she may have horrible debts or a bad credit score on paper. Sadly, if you marry that person, you will drop down with him or her on paper. Money is definitely something you should discuss before marriage. Cleaning up any unresolved bills and raising your credit score should be something else you should do before marriage. It gives both parties a fresh, healthy first step toward becoming adults in a healthy marriage.

Someone asked me if I had any advice for people who feel they need to take on debt to afford a wedding. My advice would be to take on the least amount of debt as possible. I understand you want your wedding day to be perfect. I'm going to let you in on a little secret. As long as your partner says I do and you say I do – it's perfect in every way. That's all I really wanted for my wedding, but we also celebrated it with spending money on some needs and wants. When I got married online shopping and online crafts being posted wasn't a thing. We had magazines and past weddings to get our ideas from. My wedding would of cost us so much less if we had it today. If I was newly starting my adult life and preparing to get marriage again, I would first make sure I gave us time to save for our wedding. Sit down and figure out our budget and take care of all the needs first. Cost for Church, reception hall, food and music. In

Pennsylvania, where I got married, it is very common to have your reception in a fire hall and a lot of times the caterer and bar are included in their price. So look for those places that offer package deals. It's less stress on you having to find 3 separate companies for your special day and normally is a better priced when its all in one. Next make everything you can to save on money. Also look online a lot of times people are selling amazing things they had from their wedding and at a great price. You never want to put yourself so far in debt for a wedding. I have been to several weddings that I know people spent a ton of money on and they were just ok and half those weddings, sadly those couples aren't even together anymore. Then I have also been to several weddings that friends and family pitched in with making food and making decorations and the wedding was so amazingly beautiful and it cost the people money they had in the budget without going into debt. I get it, it's your day. Sometimes splurging a little to get what you want is worth it. I really wanted a limo long enough that our entire wedding party could fit in it so no one would feel left out. That was my big top dollar thing I had to have for our wedding. We saved more money so we could make it happened. Bottom line my advice about going into debt for a wedding, I wouldn't advise it. But I understand the want for more and it being your special day. If you had to, sit down with your partner and go over a budget and figure how much in debt could you both go so paying it back monthly wouldn't hurt you guys. Take in the consideration that you may want to buy a house together in the near future, if you haven't already or one of you could lose their job or maybe you have a sweet bundle of joy coming along now too. Ultimately, you two together need to make the final decision on what will best work for you.

Now you may ask yourself how can I save money and get ahead?

I suggest putting 10% of your earnings from every paycheck into a savings account. If you feel like 10% is a lot, start small and work your way up to 10% and maybe even 20%. This next paycheck, take 2% of it and put it aside. If you bring home, say $100, take $2 from it and put it into a piggy bank or savings account. You may be laughing at $2, but I bet that $2 is an amount you wouldn't miss now, and later in life you will be glad you set aside. If you make $500 a week, 2% would be $10.

The next week, set aside 3%. $100 a week would be $3, and $500 a week would be $15.

The following week, save 4%. $100 = $4 and $500 = $20.

5% of $100 = $5 and $500 = $25
6% of $100 = $6 and $500 = $30
7% of $100 = $7 and $500 = $35
8% of $100 = $8 and $500 = $40
9% of $100 = $9 and $500 = $45
10% of $100 = $10 and $500 = $50

In one years' time, making $100 a week and saving 10% per week over the final 44 weeks, with your increase from 2%–9% over the first 8 weeks, you will have $484 in savings. Most savings accounts also make a little interest. Look into which account will do that so you can make even more.

If you are someone who makes close to $500 a week, you will save close to $2,400 a year.

That money could be used for Christmas, a vacation, a car—buying one new or repairing one—or it could help build a down payment for a house. The savings is there for when you really need it. Use it wisely, let it burn a hole in your pocket, but I suggest putting it in the savings account, or you will have to use it to buy new clothes to replace the ones with holes burned in them. Just a little financial humor there.

Say you are in your 20s, and you plan to work 'til you're in your 60s. If you made only $100 a week for the next 40 years, which is a low amount to keep making for that length of time, and if you didn't touch that money in your savings, you'd have $20,000 to help you to enjoy your senior years.

If you made $500 for the next 40 years and saved your 10%, you'd be enjoying your senior years a little better with a nice nest egg of $100,000.

And of course, the more you make, the bigger the savings. You can put it into a savings account or shop around and see where the best interest rates for your money is. There is no reason someone else should be making interest off your money, but you.

No matter what you are saving for, remember to save.

Parenting

Have you ever heard someone complain to you about how someone else parents his or her child? Have you ever complained about how someone parents a child? Has someone ever complained to you about how you are parenting?

STOP!

Stop listening to people bashing other parents, stop complaining about how people parent, and stop listening to people saying you are a bad parent.

There is no perfect parent in this world. We all screw up from time to time. What works for one child and his or her family may not be what works for you.

I have three children, and they have totally different parenting needs.

I'll give you an example among my kids as a sideline cheerleader mom. When my only daughter played sports, she didn't do well if you were screaming at her to do this or that. She did better if you sat back and watched and cheered at the appropriate times. If you sat back and watched my second child's game, so would he, instead of playing. But if you screamed and cheered for him and gave him pointers and stayed on him, he would play his heart out and outdo everyone around him. My youngest child wants no part of playing team sports or doing something his sister or brother are doing because "that's their thing." So right now, with him, we're just going with the flow. I have three kids. They all have the same parents and live in the same household, yet what motivates them—or doesn't—is different. On one day, watching the one child play, we are just the parents who sit there, watching and clapping. On another, we are "those" parents yelling at their kids to stay focused and go, go, go. I'm sure people were thinking we were hard on my middle son at those games. In my heart, I really didn't care if he won or lost, but I needed to motivate him to win, win, win because that was what he needed to succeed.

Being a parent is hard enough, so you don't need to be worrying about who thinks or said what about you or listening to negativity from others about how you are parenting.

There are times we need help parenting, but needing help and learning how to try something new with our children is different than being told we must do it a certain way.

If we all parented the same way and expected the same outcomes, we would be raising a colony of bees, and our world would fail.

I was born into this world by two teenage parents. They were constantly told what they were doing wrong.

Granted, they were doing a lot of things wrong, but instead of helping them and letting them do it the way that worked for them, they had a lot of interference from family members who felt they could do better. This probably resulted in them separating and me being pulled from both of them and bounced from one family member or family friend to another. When I lived in a home, there was always a family member outside of that home who thought they knew what was best for me, which would cause another move.

Have you ever watched how animals raise their babies? Just like humans, animal moms each raise their young differently. Some kill them (I don't recommend this action at all—just making a point), some get mean and overprotective if you get near them, some want help from humans and even from their own kind, and some do their job but really couldn't care less about what happens to their kin. We currently have two litters of kittens on our farm. The mama cats had their litters three days apart from one another. When the second litter was born, the first mama started stealing the second litter of kittens, and then the second mama stole kittens too. The first couple times we saw this, we placed the proper kittens back where they belonged. By day two both mamas had decided to put all the babies together and raise and nurse them all as one big, happy family. It was one of the sweetest things we have seen in all of our years of witnessing animal births and watching animals be raised.

We are all different, and we were all raised differently, even if we were raised in the same household. We all have our own minds with our own thoughts. We shouldn't have to feel scared or worry about people thinking we are less value than them and judging us.

I have swatted all my kiddos on their butts, when needed. Just because I used a swat for a punishment, it doesn't mean that was the punishment for everything my children did bad. I just used it when my calm, collected voice and time-outs didn't work. When my middle son was a toddler, he was not an everyday toddler, and what worked to correct him in the morning didn't work in the evening. Consistency was not key for him. His doctor even suggested we try corporal punishment (a slap on the butt, not "flogging"), which we already had. He was just different, and his brain was constantly going, and what he needed to be directed the right way was not consistent discipline. We had to daily changed our parenting for what worked in that moment, for that situation, for him.

As a parent, you will constantly question yourself or look at another mother and wonder why you aren't more like her. Don't! Don't do that to yourself. If you honestly feel you can be a better mom, then be a better mom. If you are a mom who is always doing something for your kids, don't feel bad because you kicked your feet up for an hour to eat and watch your favorite TV show, or you went out with some friends or your husband. As much as being a parent should be our number-one job, taking time out for ourselves is also important. You need that to be a better parent. Everything in life needs time to recharge. Batteries need replaced or recharged, cars need gas, and people at work need a vacation. Parents need a break from their kids every so often to be better parents. It may only be for an hour or two, but some parents need a weekend away—and it's even better when they can go together and rekindle their younger years when they were together before they had kids. No matter what the break is from parenting, take it and enjoy it and then go back and enjoy being with your kids.

I didn't mean to exclude the dads who may be reading this book. You can insert "dads" if you are one reading this.

I've had friends who call their children "monsters" or "little shi!$" or offer to sell them. Have you heard the saying, "Excuse the mess—my kids are making memories," and the derivative version, "Excuse the mess—my kids are being A$$%*@#s"? I know they are joking and wouldn't ever trade in their kids for the world, but I never understood why I wasn't like those friends who complained about their kids. I mean, my kids can be a handful. They fight everyday about something, they make a mess of my house, and sometimes they stink, lie on the couch like potatoes, are moody, etc., but I still love them. They are mine, and I am proud of them. It wasn't 'til I was driving the other day, thinking about this chapter, that I realized why I don't joke about getting rid of them or complain about them on social media or to other friends like I see with other moms. I think it's because I was that child who got passed on from family member to family friend because adults got tired of me or whatever the reason was. I have no regrets about how I was raised because it made me who I am, but I don't ever want people or my kids to think I'm throwing in the towel on them. I made my kids, and I tell them all the time that I have put in way too much of my time and energy to just get rid of them. They are my best investments. I will not let them fail.

There is nothing wrong with those parents who joke about those wild kids of theirs. I mean, my husband has offered my kids to other people before. The other day, my neighbor was telling me how when his son was a teenager, he even offered to pay people to take him. Granted, these are all joking comments, and these parents would never just give up their kids. Just make sure you remind your kids how much you love them, especially if they are hearing these comments, because they may take them seriously.

I've had several people over the years tell me what a great mom I am. I deeply love hearing that, especially on days when I feel like a horrible one or like I am failing. Being a parent is one of the hardest jobs you will ever have. It's never the same. The duties are constantly changing, and no one truly prepares you for it. It is a hands-on learning experience. What worked in the past may not work in the future. You will most likely lose your temper. If you are a mom who never yells at your kid, either you aren't parenting, or you are one lucky parent to have a saint for a child.

I homeschool my kids, so I normally always have one with me. Even now, writing this book, I hear my son in the next room chatting up a storm during his dyslexia therapy. There is no hiding from my kids. I basically live and breathe my kids. I wouldn't have it any other way. There are days when I look four years ahead, when my daughter will be off to college, my middle son will be 15, and my youngest will be 9. Then again, I look even further—seven years into the future when my daughter is turning 21, my oldest son 18, and my youngest 13. They can function on their own, hopefully. I can kick my feet up a little more often, or go to the gym in the middle of the day. I can take the dogs for a walk without having a care in the world. Unlike now where I'm always running everyone here and there. That is my dream, anyway. Then I get sad that my life will be totally different—where did my babies go? When and how did they grow up into teenagers and adults? My worries will be even worse because I won't have control over them to protect them if evil things try to hurt them. Again, being a parent will be your hardest job ever but also the most rewarding job you will ever have.

Just remember to always take a breather, kick up your feet, and spend time without kids but with your spouse or a friend. The most important thing is to be the best parent you can without worrying about what others think of you or how others are parenting.

∞ ∞ ∞

Being a Good Role Model

One day, we were driving to one of my oldest sons therapy lessons, and there was a four-way stop. Only two ways had traffic. I pulled up to the stop, and within that second, another car did too. It stopped first, so it should have gone first, then me, then the next person, and so on. When it was my turn, the car behind the first car approached the stop sign and stopped quickly, and as I drove through the intersection, he floored it. If I hadn't been paying attention to all my surroundings, we would have crashed. I laid on my horn and said, "You have got to be kidding me!" His response was to throw a hand in the air as if it were no big deal that he decided to just go because he didn't want to wait. Now, what I really wanted to do was hit the gas, fling my minivan around, hunt that guy down, and scream and yell at him about how he needs to learn how to drive and obey the laws. But of course, I had my son in the van, and we were heading to his lesson. I explain that what the guy did was wrong and could have caused an accident, and this is why it's so important to always pay attention to your surroundings when you're driving. Now, I could have been thrown into an angry mood because this guy who didn't have a care in the world almost got me into a wreck, but instead, we walked into the library, and I smiled and said, "Good morning" to a stranger and took my son to class. Being a good role model not only sets an example for the ones around you—it also sets an example for yourself and gives you a good vibe.

My husband is an amazing man and even better father. My daughter watches how he treats me, and I hope she will find a man who will treat her the same way. My oldest son sees how my husband holds open doors for people, and he follows in his daddy's footsteps by doing it too. Even when an elderly person walks slowly to the door, he will patiently wait for him or her. He's currently 10. If it's raining outside and we're running to the car, he will stand in the rain to open my door to my van to make sure I don't have to get as wet. Even my four-year-old put his hand over my head this morning during a rainstorm and told me he was trying to keep me dry while I ran with him in my arms to put him in his car seat. Our actions are always being watched. We can't just tell our kids how to be good role models. We need to be the person we want them to be.

Being a good role model isn't always for the kids to see—sometimes, it's for other adults. I can't tell you how many adults I see and think, "Really, you're an adult?" My husband never gave to the poor or needy. His philosophy was he worked hard for his money to provide for his family. There is nothing wrong with wanting to protect what you rightfully worked so hard for, especially because if you hand over money to people who you think need it, it doesn't mean they will use it wisely for food and clothing or rent. They may take the money and run with it to buy drugs, alcohol, or cigarettes. Most people have been taken advantage of too many times, and in return, this makes people very cautious about giving away something they worked hard for. Sometimes, there is a way around this, and you can still help. I never give money to a person panhandling. Instead, I ask whether he or she wants a drink or snack or hand warmers that I keep in the car for such occasions. If I get to know the person a bit better, I'll ask whether there is something they really need, such as a new shirt or shoes. The person in turn isn't wasting my money and is grateful for the little things given to him or her. In this new light, my husband has started to take an extra breakfast bar to work every morning. He told me how if it weren't for me, he'd never pay any attention to the panhandlers. Now he makes sure he can drive by them if they are out and donate a small breakfast to one. I never asked my husband to do this—he just watched me and followed my lead. My middle son is a huge follower. He's always getting everything ready for me to hand out. He will see someone at the end of the store parking lot and remind me, as we're getting into the car after shopping, that we need to go over there and give that person a snack.

My niece was visiting us this past summer, and my husband handed a drink to a panhandler, and my niece said, "We have chips in the car. See if he wants a bag of chips too." She talked about this experience afterward and was so happy we could give that man a drink and a snack.

You must learn how to balance things in your life. If you make good money and aren't living paycheck to paycheck, you need to learn how to balance that money in savings. If you can give back to someone in need, then do so. If you have children and want to make sure your retirement is secured and have money for them when they get older, then balance your future with the extra you have. Giving your extra money to the needy isn't the only answer to being a good role model. Do you have an extra hour or two or three you could spare to volunteer? Go to a nursing home, children's shelter, animal shelter, hospital, or church. Go to a place where you can help someone. Sometimes, even sitting with an elderly person for an hour and listening to everything he or she has to say is amazing. You may even learn about your history more. I remember a time my grandmother had me pick out an older gentleman sitting at the mall and to ask him about his service in the military. I sat with that older gentleman for over an hour where he told me all about how he fought in World War II. He thanked me for sitting with him and asking questions and listening and I in return thanked him for the knowledge he gave to me. It even gives you an uplifting feeling in return. This one lady at the nursing home where my daughter and I volunteer has about five sentences that she just repeats and repeats. Every time she tells me the same story, I give her a different reaction as if I'm hearing it for the first time. Would I love to hear something besides the same story over and over again? Of course! But for this lady, that's what she remembers. Think about how that could be you one day. How would you want someone to treat you? My daughter watches me with this lady and the others there at the home and sees the love I give them and wants to do the same in return. She is sad on the weeks we don't go because she wants to sit and visit with them all.

When my daughter was 11, she found out our library is always looking for volunteers to work. We were going there three times a week for therapy for my son. She signed up on her own to volunteer while we were there, cleaning toys and shelving books.

A year later, she started volunteering about four-to-eight hours a week at our vet's office because she really wants to learn from our vet and become one when she gets older. She's been there for over a year now, and they want to put her on the payroll after her next birthday. It's a good example of how volunteering is rewarding. My daughter, who has wanted to become a vet since she was little, was able to see what it was like behind the scenes at an early age, confirming her passion for her future. In doing these volunteer hours, she's being rewarded with a paying job and more hands-on learning to help her succeed in college.

I had a friend the other day tell me a story about when she had her kids with her and saw a man beating up his girlfriend as she was driving by a gas station. She could have just kept driving and minding her own business. Instead she instantly pulled over and phoned the police. Not only was she showing her kids how to be a good role model—she could have saved this woman's life.

Another friend was telling me about how a former coworker got arrested and had been in jail for some time. When people get out of jail, they've lost a lot of friends and family connections because people don't want to be associated with felons, or they were the reason they went to jail, so the person release from jail wants to distance themselves. This friend of mine, her husband and herself, opened their door to this man and his wife and has been mentoring him about life and marriage, hoping to give him enlightenment about the true worth of being here on Earth. Everyone screws up from time to time. That's part of being a human. It's what we do after our mistakes to try to better ourselves and become role models for someone else that matters.

A good way of looking at how to be a good role model is to treat others how you would want to be treated. If you work in fast food, and you are short with a customer, or you dump their fry's upside down in the bag because you don't care, you're mad, or maybe they were rude to you, that is not being a good role model. If you were the customer, would you want to be treated the way you just treated that person or his or her food?

When I was a kid, I always looked up to adults as being good role models. My family taught me that no one was better than anyone else. They taught me that a child was just as important as an adult and should be treated that way. Because of this, I never looked at adults as scary, bigger people. I looked at them as equals who I could trust as much as I did my best friend my age. Now, being taught we were all equal didn't mean I didn't have to listen to them or that I got to speak to them rudely. I still had respect, but I never felt powerless as a child. People of all ages have maturity and intelligence, which is why children shouldn't have to feel inferior to adults. It doesn't give them the right to disrespect adults, but it shouldn't hold them back from knowing more than an adult might. The brains in each and every one of us work differently. In school, for the longest time, I struggled to read and felt dumb because of it. I understood things more when they were taught by hands-on learning rather than learning from a book. I enjoyed learning when others weren't putting me down or making fun of me. It wasn't until I became an adult—a mother—and was homeschooling my two oldest kids and watching them struggle like I did that I knew something wasn't right. Like I mentioned before we were on a work trip, and on TV, they had a documentary about dyslexia. I couldn't believe it. That was ME in school. That was my kids' struggles now. After I had the two of them tested, it turned out they both had dyslexia, which is something passed down from a parent. There's a 50/50 chance that your child will inherit dyslexia. Having dyslexia, however, is amazing, and I wouldn't want to live life any other way. I never understood why, when I would explain dreams to people, they would say they didn't dream as if it's real life. It's more like a picture screen to them. It explained why I could tell why my husband's ideas wouldn't work without even trying them, while he would press forward until he tried it and saw for himself that it wouldn't work. People with dyslexia can see the images in their brain and spin it or flip it and look at it in every angle. People without dyslexia see a blueprint image and can't turn it all around or take it apart. So just because someone has a disability, it doesn't make them dumb—it just means they have to learn certain things a different way. I feel that no matter the struggles people have, they can succeed in life if they have positive people to support them. Regardless of whether people are born into the world with disabilities, if they don't have positive people helping guide and teach them, they will never be able to be the best they can be. This is why I feel that it is up to us—to you, the one reading this book—to be the role models of our future. To help strengthen the weak and teach the ones ready to learn.

Are you ready to hear an amazing secret that everyone should know? The smartest person is never done learning and will never know everything.

∞ ∞ ∞

Thinking the Grass Is Greener over There

If everything in life were handed to us, we wouldn't appreciate it as much. Did your parents ever buy you something, and you played with it but didn't take care of it? Now think about something you really wanted and had to save up to buy. After you bought it, did you play with it and toss it aside? Or did you take better care of it because you bought it with money you worked hard to get?

It's the same thing for life goals and wants. If everything we ever wanted were handed to us, we would not appreciate it. We wouldn't learn from it. We wouldn't become stronger people.

I've watched people over the years who have money—but not a lot of it—bash or be jealous of people who do. Money isn't always the answer. The richest people on this Earth struggle just as much as the poorest do. The more you make, normally the more you spend. There are good and bad in everything in life, and what we must learn is to enjoy the good and not dwell on the bad.

With social media being our world now—and I'm sure it will be a constant in our future world too—you need to ask yourself whether you want to be the one who is always posting how bad things are because you don't have the things you want. Do you want to be the person who gets anger in your stomach because you see other people online who do have them?

Let me stop your thought right there if you are one who gets jealous of what others have. Stop and take a deep breath.

> *I want you, right now, to jot down five things in your life you have that are important to you:*
> *1.*
>
> *2.*
>
> *3.*
>
> *4.*
>
> *5.*

> *Go back and read what you wrote. Now I want you to write down WHY these five things are important.*

1.

2.

3.

4.

5.

Now look at those five things and re-read why they are important. Are they important to someone else? Are they important to all your friends on social media? Probably not. They are your five most important things, and they may have the same meaning to some others, but probably not a ton of people.

In life, everyone has the things that are truly important to them. Sometimes, it's an object, a person, or something they do, such as going on vacations. No matter what it is, enjoy what is important in YOUR life and not what others have.

Financially, my family has been very blessed, but we also worked to be where we are in our lives. I lived in a mobile home as my first home at 18, and I didn't own it, I rented. I needed state assistance on my heat in the winter. There were several times I would only spend $1 a day on food and would break up one meal into three. I lived paycheck to paycheck for several years. Both my husband and I did.

There was even a moment in my life when I lived in my car between moving out of the trailer and finding an apartment.

Years later, a coworker hooked me up with her fiancé, who was a financial adviser. At that point, we took 20% of what we made—no matter how much we needed or thought we needed that money—and put it aside every paycheck. Within the year, we bought our first home. We continued holding 20% from our income for several years later.

I'm not saying there aren't families out there who honestly can't get ahead. However, most of us can, if we invest our money and don't waste it.

Do you smoke? Do you go out to bars and drink? Do you go out to eat? Do you buy stuff you truly don't need? Do you rent things, such as from a Rent-A-Center? Do you stop for those coffees on your way to work? These six things here add up to a ton of money in a months' time.

Prices are always going up and down, but I'm going to throw out some numbers based on today's numbers and the average person.

If you smoke, you spend over $2,000 a year in cigarettes. That's almost $200 a month that could be going into your savings account.

I recall a time my husband and I went out with another couple and they spent $100 on drinks alone at the restaurant. They were the same people who complained they never had money. So let's just say you drink more than some but less than others. Say you spend $200 a month in alcohol.

The average American spends $230 dollars a month eating outside the home. Multiply that number by how many people you have in your home.

Next, how much do you spend on things you don't need? Do you spend a ton of money on your hair, nails, trinkets, stuff you find cute on social media? That number can be super high or on the lower end. But honestly, figure out how much you spent in the last month on things you could LIVE without if they weren't available. When my firstborn son was a toddler, I realized I was taking him to get a haircut every 3 weeks. That was costing me $25 a month. I got my own hair cut maybe once a year, and my color from a box cost me $2.97 because I bought the lower-end kind. I still looked good and presentable. So when my oldest son was around the age two, I picked up the shaver and scissors and started cutting his hair. The first couple times, it may not have been perfect, but the more I did his hair, the better I became. Even my husband decided to stop going to the salon for haircuts, and I started to cut his hair too. Then I started to do my daughters' hair and even my own. Now I do all five of our heads in my house and probably save us, on the low end, $1,000 a year. I can't tell you how many people will compliment me or my family's great haircuts, and when I tell them, "Thanks, I cut it," they are blown away, "Oh, did you go to school for that?" Nope, I just practiced over the years. Whatever way you need to save in life, do it.

The average coffee purchase per week is $14. That's $56 a month that could be set aside for saving for a better lifestyle.

If money is tight, eat less, and eat healthier. I'm right there to gripe about how fruits and vegetables cost more than that $1.50 microwave frozen dinner or that $1 fast-food sandwich, but by eating the healthier foods, you don't have to eat as much and can be healthier and not spend a fortune on food. Buy ground coffee at the grocery store and make your own, skip the cigarettes, and shop in a smarter way.

My husband and I have seen some of our tenants rent from those Rent-A-Center places, and we want to grab our them and shake them and scream, "WHY?" They spend, on average, $150 a month for four appliances when they could have gone online and bought used stuff to start out with for about what they would pay over a month or two at rental place. You don't have to buy everything at once. My husband and I didn't buy new bedroom furniture 'til we bought our first home. Our washer and dryer were used until I became pregnant with our first child. That was the first time we bought a new washer and dryer for our home. To this day, 14 years later, we still have the same dang washer and dryer, and yes, they have had some repairs, but a new one seems to always be where my husband and I can't agree. He wants the cheapest one on the market, and I want the one probably two or three levels higher. It's kind of the joke of the family because this situation causes more fighting between my husband and me than anything else does. We didn't buy our first brand-new couch and a new nice bed mattress 'til our youngest child was on the way. We were together for 15 years when our youngest was born and before investing in new couches. We always got hand-me-downs or bought used.

We have watched several families who make way more than my husband and I do and they live paycheck to paycheck. Those same people, however, have brand-new cars, brand-new furniture, a house bigger than ours, and normally someone hired to help them clean it.

Why live a life bigger than your paycheck is? Does it truly make people happy to live such a luxurious lifestyle knowing they can't lose their jobs and don't have the option of quitting, if that job was no longer a positive environment, and still being OK? If you are living this way, you may want to change this lifestyle. Is it stressing you out having no freedom to fail or take a break?

Are you one of those people who is jealous of those living in those homes so much bigger than yours is and driving around in their brand-new cars? They may not be as happy as they appear. They may be in the same boat as you, living paycheck to paycheck. The more we make in life, the more we think we have to spend. I sometimes fall into that way of thinking—the thought of "Well, we have the money, so I'm just going to buy this and that, and oooooh, look over there at that." But the reality is I didn't need that, and I probably shouldn't have spent that money. It made me happy for a moment, but not that long.

Now jot down five things you want to make happen that take money to do or buy. Then jot down the goal you need to set to achieve them. How much does it cost? How can you achieve making the money to pay for it?

1.

Goal set to achieve:

2.

Goal set to achieve:

3.

Goal set to achieve:

4.

Goal set to achieve:

5.

Goal set to achieve:

Now set a time frame when you realistically can achieve these goals. I did this back in my early 20s. I had goals I wanted to fulfill within five years and some I gave myself 10 years for. I found that paper well over 10 years later. I had forgotten about it. I read it, and I realized as I was reading all those words and goals I had set for my future me, I had accomplished all of them. I accomplished all I wanted to on that list in the time I had planned. It's all a mindset. Sure, you are going to have setbacks and struggles along the way, but it's how we handle those setbacks and struggles that matters. My advice is to either learn from them or get back up and dust off your shoulders and be ready for them next time. Continue to keep reaching for those goals, no matter what you have to give up along the way to succeed. The harder your achievements were, the more you will appreciate them.

Are You The Receiver Or The Caller?

Are you the type of person who always texts, calls, or contacts people on social media first?

Or are you the receiver of these texts, calls, and posts instead?

Whichever you are, change your ways. If you're the go-getter person who seems to keep the bond going and going, stop and think. Does it bother you that you are always the chaser? Is it really fair that you constantly have to chase that friend down to spend time with you? Why are they not the ones calling or texting you first?

If you're the receiver, stop being lazy, thoughtless, or stuck in train of thought that you're too busy. Pick up your phone and call your friend. You make the next set of plans for getting together.

A friendship should be a two-way street. If you're the receiver, think about this friend or friends who are always there for you, calling you and checking up on you and asking you to do things. Are you the type of person who does get together when the other one asks, or do you come up with an excuse for why you can't go? Now, I'm calling you "the receiver." Let me call your friend "the caller." Now, if this caller were to die tomorrow—

maybe due to a car accident, brain hemorrhage, cancer, etc.—would you truly miss him or her? Would you wish you had spent more time with that person? If you answered "yes" to these questions, then put aside those lame excuses and figure out a way to get together—to make them feel loved as much as they love you in return. Everyone eats, even if you truly are jam packed with a busy schedule, so call your friend and let him or her know that—but say you have 30 minutes to an hour to eat lunch or dinner and that you would love it if they could join you. Anytime is better than no time.

You, the caller. Wouldn't it be great if your receiver just gave up his or her time for you to show you how much he or she appreciates you? You will not always be here, and instead of always chasing, sometimes, you just need to let go and let the wind carry you where you need to go to. Sometimes, the people we want to be number one in our lives don't deserve to be in that spot. Sometimes, the people we least expected to be there for us are the ones we should be spending time with.

Some of you may have guessed that I was the caller. I never wanted to let go of a friendship. I was constantly trying to hold onto friendships and wanting more from them. I still find myself falling back into being the caller from time to time, and then I stop and realize I just need to let them go. If they truly want to be with me and spend time with me, they will call. Maybe with certain people, you need to give them that warning that this friendship needs to be a two-way street, or it's just not going to happen. Some people truly are oblivious to how you feel. But by doing this, you actually notice who is there for you. It may only be a handful, including your spouse and kids who are really there for you. But you don't need a ton of people to live a happy life. Refocus. Maybe you are meant to spend time just finding yourself or spending time alone to soak in the outside world. Right now, you—both caller and receiver—should look up. Is it pretty outside? Even if it raining, can you go outside now? I'm asking you to put this book down now. Leave your phone, iPad, and computer all inside and just go outside for the next 15 minutes and find a spot to sit. If you smoke, this is NOT a cigarette break. It's time to just breathe. To look around. To listen. To close your eyes and remember your childhood days outside playing. This moment, right here, is all about you.

Go.

Stop reading for the next 15 minutes....

How do you feel? Are you more relaxed? Now let's have you refocused on being the caller or the receiver? Let's have you think about how you should flip the role for a bit? How maybe you should take more time to just sit and refocus on life from time to time—to soak in everything around you? If you went outside and didn't like your surroundings, maybe that is something you can also focus on. How can you change that in your life? What new goals do you need to set to make that outdoor setting be the one you want?

There are many things that make us the way we are. But we also need to realize that life doesn't revolve solely around us. We need to remind ourselves that each person out there is different. There are no two who are 100% identical in terms of what they learned in life and how they interpreted it. This knowledge should open your eyes and mind so you can realize that not everyone understands your thoughts and feelings and actions. Now that you know this, try to understand the other person and what his or her needs and wants are. Try that person's approach.

Time for an exercise.

Caller, think about your 15 minutes of outside time. What did you think about? Was there anything that reminded you of something you enjoyed besides being the caller? If not, that's OK. Think now about some hobbies you like to do or have wanted to try—possibly a store or museum you have been wanting to go to.

Now I want you to write down five things that came to mind. Over the next few weeks, every time you find yourself wanting to reach out to that person or those people, I want you to think of these five options and pick one to replace that time with.

1.

2.

3.

4.

5.

Receiver, now I want you to think about that 15 minutes outside. Did you think of anyone special? Are there people in your life who have been trying to reach out to you who you have been ignoring because you were depressed, busy, or just in your own world? I first want you to list the people around you who you know are the callers that you care about and keep blowing off. Then I want you to write down five places you would like to go and spend time with them. For the next five weeks, get a hold of your callers and make plans. Pick one of your things to do, and pick a caller. Maybe you'll choose one person or maybe a few, but no matter the number of callers you have, set a goal to reach out to them all and make a plan to spend quality time with them.

List of callers:

Places or things you would like to do with a caller:

1.

2.

3.

4.

5.

After the next few weeks, see where life takes you. See if you understand the other person just a little bit more. If you're the caller, I hope you will find there's more to life than feeling like you have to be the one who keeps the relationship going. Maybe you'll find out you have others who you didn't even realize were there who needed you just as much as you needed someone to need you. Maybe you found out that enjoying a hobby is what you needed to relax and refocus your thoughts. If you're the receiver, I hope you will enjoy the fact that you became the caller and see how much it meant to the former callers when you made the first move. I hope you will appreciate how you filled a need for them and that you will come to enjoy being the caller at times. Both the caller and receiver, I hope you learned about balance and how to enjoy your daily lives just a little bit more. Hopefully, you can continue what you've learned over the last five weeks and continue it into your life to keep the balance.

Menopause

Some of you readers are probably thinking, "What? I'm nowhere near the age for that." Maybe you are already past that stage. Or maybe you are wondering why are we talking about menopause after talking about marriage, money, kids, friends, and life? Well, because it's part of life. Whether this is part of your life now, approaching, already past, or nowhere near, or maybe you are a guy—and if you are a guy, this will probably still be a good chapter for you to read because anytime a male can understand a woman more, it will just make your life easier.

Remember that we are all different, and no one will ever 100% agree with you because we all experience different things in our lives. No two lives are the same. Even if two people are raised in the same household and experience the same thing, it doesn't mean they took the same things from those experiences.

I'm a firm believer that things happen for a reason, good and bad. So I take all of that and learn from it. Another person may take those bad experiences and dwell on them and feel pain, shame, or hatred.

In the summer of 2018, I had the worst chest pains. I honestly thought I was having a heart attack. So, of course, I was rushed to the hospital in the middle of the night. They ran tests on me and found nothing wrong with me. But I still felt off. The next day, I experienced the same thing and once again ended up back at the hospital, and I was again sent home with nothing wrong with me. I followed up with my primary-care physician (PCP), and he scheduled me for a stress test and did some more bloodwork. Still nothing. A month went by, and I got my period for the second time in the same month. I was so tired. I took my boys to the dentist, and I started having hot flashes. I mean, it was uncontrollable sweating and burning up, and did I mention sweating? You feel wet like you just got out of the pool. I was drinking the cold water bottles the dentist had just to try to cool myself down. This was the moment I realized I must be going through menopause, even though I was in my early 40s. However, I didn't put two and two together and attribute what had felt like a heart attack to menopause.

Things started to get worse for me. I became depressed. I couldn't shake this feeling. There was nothing in my life causing me to be depressed. This time was any eye-opener to me, though. That's why I wanted to add this chapter to the book.

I've always been a firm believer that you can control your brain to think positive thoughts. If you are depressed, there's a reason for it. You are thinking of something bad that happened to you.

Well, in my case, the depression I was feeling wasn't being brought on by anything besides the menopause causing a chemical imbalance in my brain. This was when I realized why some moms who lived happy, carefree lives just snapped and hurt someone they loved or themselves.

Over and over again, I kept thinking I needed to get a gun and shoot myself in the head to end my life. The thought was so intriguing that it was making me feel like it was really a good idea. That I should really just get up, get a gun, load it, and shoot myself. It made as much sense to me as when I want to go make a sandwich when my body tells me I'm hungry.

Luckily, I am strong-willed and do think things out before reacting. I started to question myself. Why did I think this was such a great idea? Nothing was wrong in my life at that moment. Everything was great. Why would I think it would be OK to just shoot myself so my kids and or husband could find my dead body and have to live with that image in their brains for the rest of their lives?

I didn't really want to shoot myself, and I really didn't want to die. I didn't even have anything that was bothering me that I wanted to get away from so I wouldn't have to deal with it. It all made no sense. In fact, because none of it made sense, I kept it to myself because I was embarrassed I felt that way with no explanation.

I also was so short-tempered with everyone in the house, and everything either made me cry or scream. I had no control over my body anymore.

I finally started to feel a little better after about two weeks, and I spoke to a girlfriend who had stopped by who actually deals with depression herself. She understood my emotions. I felt like maybe I shouldn't be so embarrassed by what was going on. I thought that maybe I should open up about it and take control before it took control of me. A few nights later, I told my husband what had been going on in my brain and in my body, how I felt, and how I hated feeling as if I weren't in control of my emotions and thoughts. Thankfully, I have a loving husband who told me he felt sad that he didn't know what I was going through. He said I should always know I can confide in him about anything.

A month later, my family and I went to Texas for a few days, and while the older kids and my husband were at a baseball game, the youngest and I stayed back at the motel because he didn't want to go. I decided I would do some more research on menopause while he watched TV. I came across an amazing article that Oprah Winfrey wrote. She talked about how she awoke in the middle of the night to her heart palpitating so intensely that it felt like it was going to beat right out of her chest. She thought she was going to die. For six months, her doctors all told her she was fine after tests upon tests had been run on her. She went running with her trainer one morning and told him about what was going on, and he said it was probably the big M. She was 47 at the time. She mentions how she came across a book called *The Wisdom of Menopause*. I have actually ordered this book, but I'm still waiting for its arrival.

The reason I told you all to continue to read this is because even if you are not near menopause or are a guy who will never get it, I wanted you to learn about it and be aware of the ladies in your life who may be going through this or will in the future. Don't take an outburst from them to heart. Now that you have learned the signs, maybe you can be a little sympathetic toward them. Help them around the house. I will tell you, the worn-out tiredness is just as bad as having the flu, minus the sickness part.

What we all need to remember though is this is LIFE, and THAT'S Okay!

∞ ∞ ∞

We Are Daily Growing

I'm going to end this book with this chapter because I think this is probably one of the most important things we need to know for ourselves and about others. We are daily growing. Did you know that? You're probably thinking, "Yes, I did." But when you think of daily growing, you are probably thinking about being born as a baby, toddlerhood, being a child, being a teenager, adulthood, and becoming a senior. But that's not the daily growing I am talking about.

When you were a young child, you may have been a hair puller, pitcher, or biter (which that was me—oh, how I loved to bite people), or maybe you would take toys from others because sharing was hard. I bet you didn't grow up into your teens and adulthood and still pull other people's hair, pitch people, or bite them, and you probably learned to share. We are always growing, and our brain is always learning, and we learn from our mistakes to make us better people.

Learning about right and wrong as a young child helped you grow into a civilized person. However, that isn't the only thing I want you to take from this chapter.

I wanted to explain that so you can see we are always learning and changing.

In my life, I had people who weren't the best role models for me. People who I really was mad at because they weren't more to me, or I didn't mean more to them. People who I thought when I became an adult and I could make my own decisions that I would choose not to have them in my life anymore because of actions and decisions they made toward me as a child and young adult.

Sometimes, in our young lives, we are being protected by others from certain mistakes our role models made. Sometimes, our role models, the ones we look up to and cling to their every word as truth, tell us untrue stories about people who are trying to be good role models to us to make the one telling us the story to look better. This can get complicated and sticky. Making the right decision can be a blur at times.

You just need to learn to open your eyes and ears and listen to all the stories and use your eyes to watch these people. You need to make the call of whether someone is a good role model for you and not let others persuade you one way or another.

My mom and I didn't have a very close bond when I was a child. I even remember, when I was two, making her frustrated with me when she and my dad were married. When they separated when I was around three, I was sent off to live with family and friends. I remember my frustrated feelings toward my mother increased, and I wished I never had to see her again. I felt she didn't want me, that I was a burden to her, where my dad always wanted to see me when he could and always wanted to do things with me. My other family members took me places, played games with me, and seemed to always want me around. I never felt that love come from my mother. This was my observation as a child learning about life. I was raised in a way that wasn't the normal family with mom, dad, and siblings. I was living as a child from a teenage pregnancy who got bounced from house to house between family and friends 'til I was 18. There were seven different families, between family and friends and different homes, that I can recall. Family members and friends all thought they had the best answer to what would work best for Angela and wanted to give it a try. Basically, a few reasons of why I was bounced from one home to another was because most felt sorry for me. Most put things in their own head to make them think they could be the one who could save me from not growing up to be a nobody. Some could handle certain ages well and others couldn't handle certain ages like the teen years. Of course, there were people in my life who had true intentions of wanting what was best for me. I also feel that in some situations that if someone thought they could benefit having me live with them, they fought for me to move in with them. In the long run I actually learned so much living with all these people, all these lifestyles. I went from families that didn't even talk about God to another one that went to church three times a week. I changed a lot from each home I was living in and learned all the good and bad from them.

During all this time I was growing into an adult, my mother wasn't a big part of my life. I felt closer to her mother—my grandmother—than I did to her. When my maternal grandmother got sick, she tried to start mending the relationship between my mother and me, but we weren't there yet. My mother still needed to grow more, and I needed to learn that it's life, and THAT'S Okay, and not hold on to the resentment I had toward her.

In fact, I really wasn't even going to write this chapter because I didn't want to throw anyone under the bus. Nevertheless, I think this chapter is very important because people are dealing with odd situations like this or not understanding things in life, and they need to hear it. Not necessarily with their mother, like I'm going to discuss—it could be another family member or friend or spouse. What I want you to take from this chapter is that we are always learning.

Over my young adult years my mother was a come-and-go type of mother. Every time I thought she was there, she was gone. I wanted her to be a part of my life. I wanted her to love me like I was the most important thing in her life. Yet it never seemed to happen the way I wanted, so I pushed her away. If she wasn't chasing after me, why should I chase after her? Thus, we just both started to live our own lives. To grow for ourselves. She graduated from college with a bachelor then went back for her masters, and I met the love of my life and started my adulthood with marriage.

After my wedding, she tried again to be a better mom, though it wouldn't be 'til four years later, when my husband and I had our first child and made my mom a grandmother, that I saw the biggest change in her. I saw her step to the plate. I watched her be a grandmother to my kids the way I wanted to her to be a mother to me, and it made all my pain I had carried through the years of feeling abandoned by her all go away. My kids are the most important things in my life, and anyone who is there for my kids means more to me than if they were there for me.

If it weren't for the longing I wanted from my mother growing up, I don't think I would be as good of a mother as I am to my kids. My children are my world, and I never want them to feel abandoned or unloved. I never want them to feel the way I felt.

Every year, my mother and I have been growing closer and closer the older we get. Every time we see each other, the better it gets. She is not the same teenager who got married because she was pregnant with me. She is not the same young adult who didn't put me first. She is now a grandmother who loves her grandkids and spends time with them. She spoils them and spends time with me when we can. And she actually wants to do it.

I'm not saying that everyone is going to change for the better. I'm also not saying that if you have cut certain people out of your life to make it better or healthier just to let them back in. I am, however, reminding you that "YES! People do change. YES! People do learn."

Sometimes, in our lives, we have been hurt over and over and over again by certain people, and some of us take it to heart so much that it breaks us. Please, if you are the one getting broken, don't let another person break you. Know that it's not you, and that the person breaking you needs to grow up more. But when you give that person time to grow, know that he or she may have truly changed into the person he or she always wanted to be—the person you always wanted him or her to be. Sometimes, it's worth giving people second and third and even fourth chances.

Now, every circumstance is different, so use this advice wisely.

And if you are the person who was the one cut out, you need to understand you may have hurt that person so much that he or she just can't open his or her heart again to you.

If that is the case, you both just need to learn from the past and be the best version of yourselves that you can be to the ones who are currently around you.

Life isn't always easy, especially if we don't understand it.

Things in life happen.

We all just need to understand not to judge others, to listen to what is being said around us, to watch others, and to try being the best we can be. That is when we can achieve a proficiency of knowledge and understanding of life.

It's LIFE, and THAT'S Okay

Notes:

Made in the USA
Coppell, TX
05 November 2020